GREEN HOME

the joy of living with plants

ANDERS RØYNEBERG

GREEN HOME

the joy of living with plants

Anders Røyneberg (@arcticgardener)
Written in collaboration with Erik Schjerven

Hardie Grant

QUADRILLE

Contents

People have always been interested in plants, and there are botanical gardens all over the world. The Botanical Garden in Oslo is my favourite.

TO MUM AND DAD, THE NURSE AND THE FARMER WHO TAUGHT ME A LOVE OF PEOPLE AND NATURE

FOREWORD

"What's so great about having so many plants?"

That's the question I'm often asked on Instagram, where I go under the name @arcticgardener.

It may seem a bit crazy having 100 houseplants in a small apartment – I can see that. But I do have a philosophy underlying this green extravagance. Plants are good for me – in more ways than one: I'm inspired by their beauty, happy that they produce oxygen and purify the air around me and they make me feel calmer. Research shows that plants can improve mental well-being.

"Isn't it horribly complicated?"

No, it doesn't have to be – even though we Norwegians live in the frigid north, and even though all of us (including me!) have a number of plant deaths on our conscience. Over time I've learned one or two things about caring for plants that I'd like to share with you. You don't have to go out and get 100 plants, but surely you can manage one, maybe two ... or even more?

A few years ago, when I started posting images of
my green apartment on Instagram, the response was
overwhelming. Why was that? I believe the main reason
is that we humans depend on plants for our well-being.
I'm also aware that a lot of plant people are keen on
caring for the planet. That's why I describe myself as
pro-plant and pro-planet – there's a connection there.

My hope is that this book will inspire you to become
a plant enthusiast. You might be interested in houseplants
because they're beautiful and they can brighten up an
interior; perhaps you're more interested in the health
benefits – or like me, you're interested in both aspects.

Whatever your motivation, I have a number of tips and
some advice that I would like to share: what plants you
should choose, how to look after them, how they can
bring something to an interior and what health benefits
you'll enjoy. My aim is to help you to like plants even
more. So, I hope you have a plant-astic read!

PLANT PEOPLE ARE PEACEFUL PEOPLE

If you like plants, I would like to start by saying – congratulations, you're clearly not a troublemaker! Plant people are peaceful people, and just the fact that you're leafing through this book is a good sign. Plant people are not into hassle and strife. We'd rather have peace and quiet where we look after our plants.

A green, global force

Plant people all over the world have something in common: love of, and respect for, plants. There's a global force at work, and we're growing in number – people who think that plants aren't just decorative, but are a vital part of our lives. The green wave is washing over the globe. You might think I sound naïve, and possibly that's true. I'm no extremist – I eat meat now and again and I take flights – but at the same time I have a firm belief that plants, whether they're growing in the home or in the Amazon, will be one of the most important things that we need to look after in the years to come. With their ability to produce oxygen, plants breathe life itself!

Maybe you've heard about the green shift? People all over the world are craving a closer connection to nature, living more in and with the green world – and the growing number of houseplant owners is symbolic of this longing. For a long time, many of us have become increasingly divorced from the natural world, but now we're taking it back – and into our homes. My hope then is that more and more people will be inspired to turn their living spaces into green oases.

We humans feel better when we're living close to nature. I call it the power of chlorophyll, the very reason why we are now seeing more people filling their homes with plants. Houseplants make us healthier, calmer and more balanced. Alternative? No. Scientific? Yes.

Young people want to live greener lives. They respond proactively to news about the risks of plastic in the sea, pesticides on food, polluted air and global warming. Houseplants have played an important role in this awakening: for example, more and more school children are now learning to sow, tend and harvest indoor greens. In a few years, we will have raised a committed army of green soldiers eager to spread the green evangelism, and the thought makes my green heart glad.

#jegelskerplanter [#iloveplants]

… and that's why I have 100 of them in my tiny Oslo apartment. I've got banana plants, citrus plants, olive trees, ferns, tropical plants, succulents and much, much more. Some of my friends think I have a problem, that my passion for plants has gone a bit too far – but I tell them there are worse things. I still think I've got it under control. For some time, I've been working at giving plants away. It's tough, but I'm getting there. Plants are addictive – you are hereby warned!

My interest in plants started when I was just a child. I grew up on a farm, surrounded by countryside, with my mum and dad and five sisters – we're a big family. I'm proud of my sisters. They're all strong, independent Nordic women who aren't afraid of getting stuck in. A lot of people assume that as the only boy in this female environment I must have been spoiled rotten, but I wasn't. I'd actually say that it toughened me up. Mum and dad taught us the importance of social equality, that all people are of equal value. We had a good and fair upbringing that was also close to nature, and memories of playing in green meadows still make me feel sentimental.

When I moved to Oslo, it left a void. I loved the life and bustle of the capital and its opportunities, but there was still something missing. Before long I started to fill my home with more and more plants. There was a need to recreate what I had left behind a connection to my own childhood. I could have just moved back, but instead I chose to bring the natural world into my city apartment. I found the greener I made my space, the more my restlessness abated.

CHOOSING THE RIGHT PLANT

Let's get straight to the point. My main rule for success is to go for robust plants, and fortunately there are quite a few to choose from. The second most important consideration is, as a general rule, to select plants that can survive what I call the "three months of death": November, December and January. In Norway, this is the season when we have very short days and natural light is a scarce commodity, and as a result a lot of houseplants die. Even the UK, which is slightly further south, has only just over seven hours of daylight on the shortest day. So how can you get your plants to survive, and even thrive, all year round?

Essential for success: go for robust plants that suit the light conditions in your home. Why? Light is important for plants to grow and to flourish.

Plants with light-coloured leaves need lots of light.

Plants with dark leaves need less light.

While some succulents and cacti are true sun lovers, many prefer indirect, bright light and some will even tolerate lower light levels.

By far the easiest plants for a lot of people are succulents and cacti, which store water in their leaves and stems and require minimal care.

Thick and fleshy dark green leaves

The most important rule of thumb is to choose a plant with thick leaves. These are plants that store water in their leaves, so they can go without care and watering for fairly long periods. In fact, they can even be neglected to a degree, which makes them perfect for people who travel a lot or who forget about their plants from time to time.

Some of these are desert plants that survive by retaining water during dry periods. They store water in their leaves because they know that it might be a while before they can enjoy the next downpour. As a result, desert plants don't like to be over-watered, as that can cause their roots to rot. They like owners who are stingy with water. I really enjoy watering, so these plants can be a bit of a challenge for me.

So what should you actually do when buying plants? Feel the leaves! If they are thick and with a solid consistency, they are good at storing water. This means that you can go away for a few weeks without worrying too much about their dying of thirst.

Dark leaves may be a sign that the plant can cope without much light. A lot of these manage pretty well with the "death months".

My easy-care favourites
- Emerald palm (*Zamioculcas zamiifolia*)
- Fishbone cactus (*Epiphyllum anguliger*)
- Mother-in-law's tongue (*Sansevieria trifasciata*)

Easy-care favourites from my followers on Instagram
- Fiddle-leaf fig (*Ficus lyrata*)
- Golden pothos (*Epipremnum aureum*)
- Rubber plant (*Ficus elastica*)
- Spider plant (*Chlorophytum comosum*)
- Spineless yucca (*Yucca elephantipes*)
- Swiss cheese plant/Monstera (*Monstera deliciosa*)
- Waxflower (*Hoya*)

HANDY HINT

Choose robust plants with thick, dark green leaves but, most importantly, start with the light conditions in your home.

There's a plant to suit everyone

Your lifestyle and personality are all-important factors for what plant you might succeed with. Which plant do you most recognize yourself in?

The starter If you're completely green when it comes to plants, get a robust plant that is easy to look after. Suggestion: emerald palm (*Zamioculcas zamiifolia*)

The plant serial killer Are you a serial killer with a whole lot of plant deaths on your conscience? If that sounds like you, then you need to get a plant that's difficult to kill. Suggestion: mother-in-law's tongue (*Sansevieria trifasciata*)

The jet-setter Are you a jet-setter with a busy job, lots of travel and the joys of the gravy train? Not home that often? You need an independent plant – get yourself a cactus. Suggestion: fishbone cactus (*Epiphyllum anguliger*)

Busy parents with young children If your job, children, clubs and activities all make demands on your time, you should go for robust plants that can tolerate some neglect. Suggestion: areca palm (*Dypsis lutescens*)

The caring owner Do you like spending time with your plants – checking up on them, talking to them, tidying them up and tending to them a lot? Suggestion: calathea (*Calathea orbifolia*). This green, tropical beauty has a few needs, but is strikingly attractive. Definitely my favourite.

The smart one If you have the horticultural smarts, then go for a challenge. Suggestion: maidenhair fern (*Adiantum*). If you can manage this, then you know what you're doing! Although exceptionally pretty, its need for plenty of watering, misting, plant food and light demands a lot of its owner.

Fear of failure has prevented me from getting one of these – but perhaps it's time for me to try?

The plant nerd Are you one of those nerdy types who likes plants that are unusual or a bit different? Do you also like to experiment and read up on plants and their various needs? Suggestion: avocado plant (*Persea americana*). To start producing your own home-made avocado plant, buy an avocado from the shop, eat it and put the stone in water – it's that easy (see page 29).

The fashionista Obsessed by trends? Get a Swiss cheese plant (*Monstera deliciosa*). Having said that, that was last year's trend ... How about a false shamrock (*Oxalis triangularis*)? If you're an on-trend plant person, there is the risk of having to replace your plants – big time. Probably best to just choose a plant you like.

The gourmand If you like to eat your plants, then there's a veritable sea of green herbs that you can grow indoors year-round. Suggestion: parsley (*Petroselinum crispum*). If you put a small plant cultivation light or an LED light beneath your kitchen cabinet, you'll be able to harvest fresh parsley year-round and add it to your meals straight from the pot.

The health-conscious If you're concerned about the air quality in your home, get yourself a real air filter, such as golden pothos (*Epipremnum aureum*). This will help to remove contaminants from your interior air so that you can feel healthy and energized, have better skin and enjoy better sleep.

Light conditions are everything

It was an epiphany for me when I realized how important light conditions were for my plants. It's essential to select plants based on the light available in your home. In order to succeed and for your plants to be able to thrive, you have to establish how much light your home gets. Do your windows face north, south, east or west?

The plants in my partner's loft apartment in the Grünerløkka district of Oslo are absolutely flourishing. They get light from above through the skylights, just like in a forest where plants grow beneath tall trees. Maybe they do so well here because the light from above reminds them of their original habitat somewhere in the Amazonian jungle? In my own apartment in the St. Hanshaugen district all the windows are east-facing, with moderate sunlight. (For more on light conditions, see pages 38–45.)

Plants that cope with little light
- Dragon tree (*Dracaena marginata*)
- Emerald palm (*Zamioculcas zamiifolia*)
- Fishbone cactus (*Epiphyllum anguliger*)
- Golden pothos (*Epipremnum aureum*)
- Swiss cheese plant/Monstera (*Monstera deliciosa*)

Plants that need light
- Cacti (several species)
- Calamondin (*citrus x microcarpa*)
- Elephant's foot (*Beaucarnea recurvata*)
- Succulents (several species)
- Umbrella plant (*Schefflera*)
- Spineless yucca (*Yucca elephantipes*)

FACT

Even the darkest corner outdoors is lighter than the lightest corner indoors. Whereas outdoor light floods in from all directions, Indoor light comes from just one point – your window. South-facing windows provide the most light.

Most smart phones have a compass that you can use to find out which direction your home faces.

Where can you buy houseplants?

I buy my plants from various places. You will find the best-quality plants in a proper plant shop, plus I always like to support local plant shops that employ dedicated professional staff. They'll also be able to give you tips and advice on which plants are right for you and how to look after them.

I'm not a fanatic, so I buy my plants here and there. If I like something, more often than not I'll yield to temptation. You can also find plants everywhere from nurseries to grocery stores. I was once told off by a committed flower shop owner who told me that I had "sold my soul to the dark forces" by buying plants at IKEA. Plants bring out passionate feelings in people.

WHAT PLANTS DO YOU GO FOR?
When looking for plants, go for the ones with strong, green, healthy and robust leaves, and avoid those with yellow, red or brown patches on their leaves. A weak and brittle stem can also be a sign that there is something wrong. Pests are often visible, so do a thorough check to see that the plant is free from insects, both on top of and underneath the leaves. However, if the plant has been trimmed in the shop, for example if the top shoot has been removed, this isn't usually a bad sign, as plants sometimes become damaged during transport to the shop.

ARE PLANTS POISONOUS?
Both children and house pets may find it exciting to touch and taste plants. Most houseplants are not poisonous, but the sap of some plants may irritate the skin, mouth, throat and stomach. Swallowing the sap may cause discomfort, such as itching and stomach ache. If an accident does happen, the recommendation is to rinse your mouth and drink plenty of water – cold dairy products such as yoghurt can also reduce discomfort. If symptoms are severe, you should see a doctor.

Plants with irritating sap
- Emerald palm (*Zamioculcas zamiifolia*)
- Orchids (several species)
- Peace lily (*Spathiphyllum wallisii*)
- Knight's star lily/Amaryllis (*Hippeastrum*)
- Alocasia (*Alocasia*)
- Hortensia/Hydrangea (*Hydrangea macrophylla*)

GETTING STARTED

Having got to the point of acquiring a plant that's right for you and your lifestyle, and checking the light conditions in your home, in principle all you need is soil and a suitable pot.

SOIL TYPES FOR POTTED PLANTS

In my experience, a good potting compost works fine for most plants. A lot of shops advertise different kinds of potting compost, so-called specialist composts, but this is often just an unnecessary expense.

Although most plants do fine in potting compost, cacti and succulents do best in sandy compost that drains well and doesn't hold moisture. Use seed and cactus compost as it contains fewer nutrients, has more sand and allows excess water to drain away quickly.

DIFFERENT TYPES OF POT

The vast majority of plants prefer pots made from natural materials that breathe, such as terracotta pots made from clay. Plants that like constantly moist soil, such as papyrus and ferns, will do fine in plastic pots, while cacti and succulents prefer clay pots, because natural materials dry out faster and prevent the build-up of excess moisture in the soil.

You may decide to leave the plant in the plastic pot that it came in when you bought it, but it's best to repot it immediately into a pot that's one size bigger. That should give your plant a good start.

GOOD DRAINAGE

Do you need to put leca balls (baked clay balls) or pebbles in the bottom of the pot? No, you don't have to do anything, but in my experience leca balls will double the chances of the plant doing well. The reason? The leca balls make sure that any excess water drains away, so the plant roots are better aerated. This prevents root rot, one of the most common causes of plants dying. So yes, go for leca balls or pebbles in the bottom of the pot, and maybe mix some leca balls into the compost as well. If you do that, your plant will thrive – and maybe reward you with a fresh, new leaf now and again.

PROPAGATION

all about seeds, suckers, leaf cuttings and stem cuttings

You can of course buy plants, receive them as gifts or acquire them as part of a plant exchange, but what I enjoy most is producing my own "heirs" from a parent plant. This is particularly true if there's a plant that I'm really fond of, and which I'm worried might not survive.

There are various methods for propagating from your plant collection: from seed, from leaf and stem cuttings and from suckers, or pups. Spring and summer are the best seasons for propagating. That's when the plant is going at full speed into the growing season – perfect for making new baby plants!

GIFT IDEA

The best present to give and to receive? A home-made plant! You'll also be making a gift of the time and love you have invested in the plant to someone you care about. The recipient is guaranteed to be even happier than you!

Golden pothos

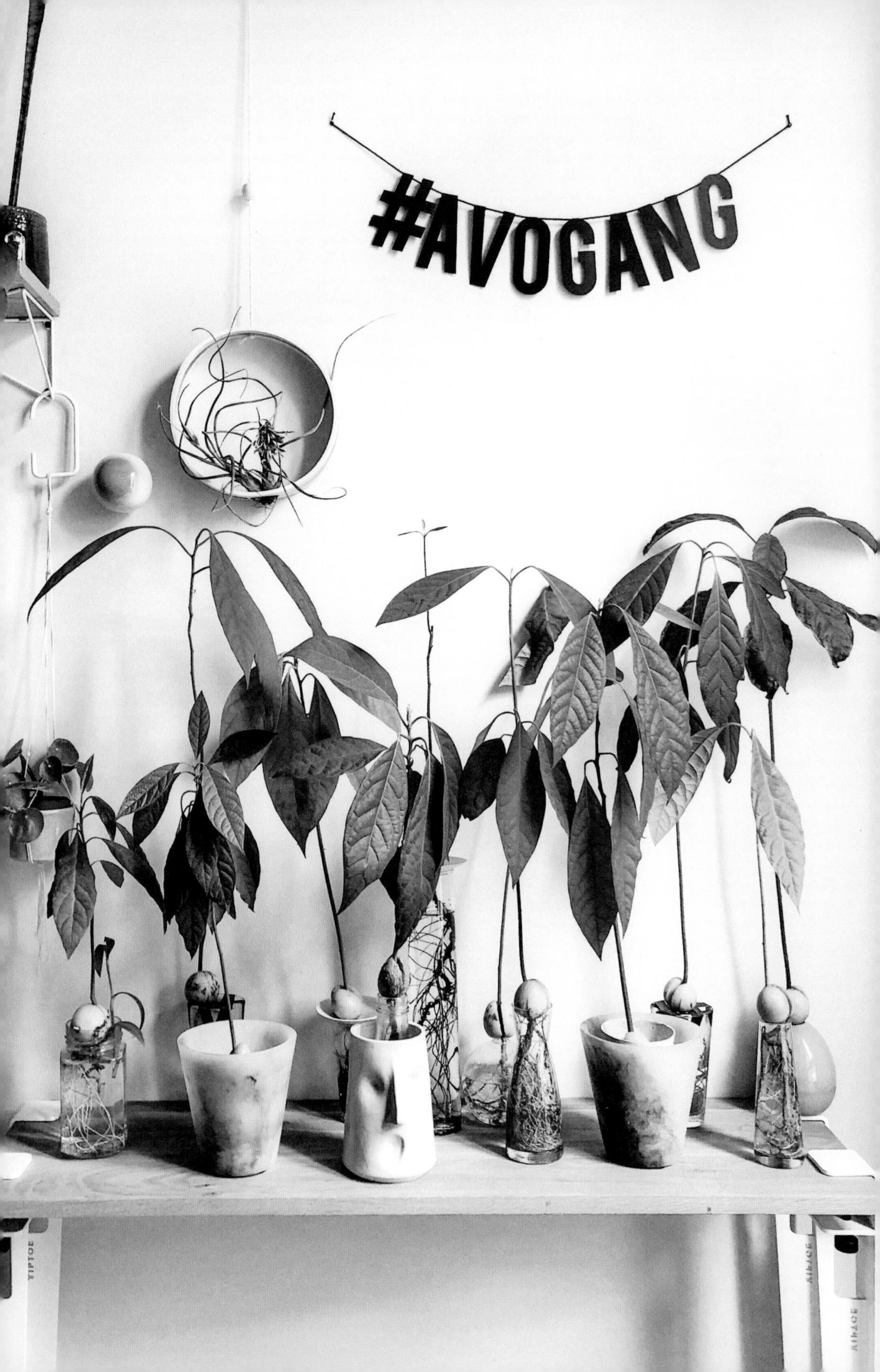
#AVOGANG

Seed

Most plants can be cultivated from seed, but some are easier to succeed with than others. If you're growing from seed, the best time to do this is in spring, right at the start of the growing season.

AVOCADO

The avocado plant (*Persea americana*) has become really popular recently as a houseplant. The actual process of cultivating it is just so easy, educative and interesting. Here are the instructions for how, having eaten an avocado, you can use the seed (also called the stone) to cultivate your own avocado tree. Good luck!

1 Wash the stone and remove any remaining fruit.

2 Holding the narrow end upwards, stick four pins into the stone about 2cm (¾in) from the top (a lot of people achieve good results with toothpicks).

3 Fill a clear glass with water, and put the stone in it with the pins resting on the rim of the glass.

4 Check that the bottom of the stone is beneath the water level at all times.

5 Put the glass in the sunniest spot in your home. The avocado is originally from Central and South America and it likes a lot of sun.

6 Change the water a few times each week to stop the stone going mouldy.

7 After a few weeks, the stone will split and put roots down into the water.

8 After a few more weeks, you'll see a shoot start to sprout from the top of the stone.

9 Once the shoot has grown to about 20cm (8in) in height, pot it up in some potting compost, with the top part of the stone sitting slightly above the surface of the compost.

10 The avocado plant must be kept moist, as it's thirsty and likes plenty of water. Don't forget to use a pot with a hole and drainage so that it doesn't drown!

FACT

Unfortunately, growing conditions in northern Europe aren't good enough to produce avocado fruit, unless you have particularly good growing conditions in your home – but with its long stems and large oval leaves, it is an attractive and interesting plant.

Leaf cuttings

A lot of plants can be propagated from the leaves of the parent plant, especially those with thick leaves, such as succulents, which are ideal for taking leaf cuttings. Summer is a good time to do this.

SUCCULENTS

How to propagate succulents from leaf cuttings.

1 Use seed and cactus compost. You don't need a deep pot.

2 Water the surface of the compost.

3 Cut leaves from the parent plant, either gently by hand or by using a clean, sharp knife, ideally selecting ones located at the base of the plant.

4 Place the leaves on the potting compost with the cut edge in contact with the surface of the compost.

5 Keep the surface of the compost moist by spraying it with water a few times a week.

6 After three to four weeks, you'll notice small roots forming, and eventually small rosettes.

7 Using a spoon, transfer the cuttings to larger pots, where they can grow bigger.

Stem cuttings

I enjoy taking and giving cuttings – these are small sections cut from the stems of plants that will grow up to become new plants in their own right.

GOLDEN POTHOS (*Epipremnum aureum*) **AND SILVER VINE** (*Scindapsus pictus*)
Taking stem cuttings is easy, and some plants are easier to succeed with than others, such as golden pothos and silver vine.

1 Using a pair of secateurs, cut off one of the plant's branches just below a node (the bumps you can see on the stem) and strip off the lower leaves.

2 Put the cutting in a clear glass or a bottle with some water.

3 Replace the water weekly.

4 After about two to six weeks the cutting will develop roots.

5 Plant the cutting in some potting compost.

HANDY HINT

If you see a good-looking plant at a friend's place, why not take a cutting? It's usually best to ask, but I have been known to take a sucker or two without asking. One of my golden pothos plants came from a petrol station in Ringerike, a region northwest of Oslo.

The small, brown nodes are where new stems and leaves form on a plant. However, once cut and the stem cutting placed in water the nodes put their energy into forming new roots instead.

Silver vine (*Scindapsus pictus*)

Suckers

Suckers are small plants, often referred to as pups, that grow out from the parent plant and put out roots, or send out runners on long stems that run along the ground. These pups can be cut and separated from the root system of the parent plant and put in their own pots, where they develop into new plants – which then go on to produce baby plants of their own.

CHINESE MONEY PLANT (*Pilea peperomioides*)
Taking suckers from a Chinese money plant is easy.

1 Find a sucker and carefully remove the soil from around it. Dig down as deep as you need to.

2 Using a clean, sharp knife, carefully cut the sucker off as far down as you can without damaging the roots of the parent plant.

3 Clean off the soil and put the sucker in a small clear glass or jar with some water. After a few weeks to a few months, it will develop roots. The sucker can then be planted in some potting compost.

4 You can also try planting the sucker directly in compost and hope that it will manage to put down roots. This approach usually works out fine, although short cuts can sometimes end up in disaster.

Make your own *Pilea* family. As this plant is easy to propagate, you can quickly create your own *Pilea* baby plants. *Pilea* suckers also make perfect gifts for friends and family.

CARE

Anyone can have green fingers – even those who consider themselves notorious plant serial killers. All that's needed is interest, a little knowledge and some experience. So how can you get a plant to thrive under your care? The first thing is to understand the three basic needs of plants: light, water and nutrients.

LIGHT

Plants make their own building materials by using light in a process called photosynthesis, so the more you optimize the lighting conditions, the more energy the plants receive – and the more they will flourish.

WATER

Water is essential for life, both for plants and for people – this combination of hydrogen and oxygen is responsible for all life on earth. Without water, plants dry up, while too much water drowns them. Mastering watering is therefore essential to get plants to thrive.

NUTRIENTS

Just like us humans, plants need a supply of nutrients in order to stay healthy. This is why we give plants plant food – or fertilizer, as it's often called. Plant food stimulates growth and so makes plants healthier and more robust while boosting flowering.

PRACTICAL ADVICE ABOUT LIGHT

I started out by getting a whole load of plants that needed a lot of light, but in the absence of sufficient light they said their goodbyes and promptly died. It was only when I realized that I would need to get plants that could survive in my east-facing windows (i.e. with only moderate levels of sunlight) that I saw the light – quite literally.

THE RIGHT PLANT FOR THE LIGHTING CONDITIONS IN YOUR HOME

The amount of light available in your home will determine how much success you'll have with your plants. Most plants prefer plenty of indirect light, in other words, plenty of light but usually not direct sunlight.

Use the following as a general rule of thumb:

• South-facing window
Plenty of available light

• West-facing window
Plenty-to-moderate levels of available light

• East-facing window
Moderate-to-low levels of available light

• North-facing window
Low levels of available light

HANDY HINT

You don't actually need windows and natural light to grow plants. For instance, if you have a windowless bathroom, you can still use lighting that will ensure happy and healthy plants year-round. Ceiling full-spectrum fluorescent lighting will work fine. A full-spectrum LED light is also suitable (see also page 44). Tropical plants such as calathea thrive in warm bathrooms with moisture from showers and washing, as these conditions remind them of their home in the tropics.

SOUTH: plenty of sunlight

Desert plants such as cacti and succulents want sun, light and heat, and can tolerate plenty of all three. They'll thrive year-round in south-facing windows.

Most houseplants will also do well in a south-facing window, but they'll need some protection from the sunlight in spring and summer. During these seasons, you can move them a bit away from the window, into the room or to one side of the window, so that they're in half-shade. You could also protect them using a sheer curtain.

WEST AND EAST: sunlight and half-shade

A window in either of these directions will provide moderate levels of light, which most plants prefer. During the colder months, plants can be left directly in the window – whereas during the warmer months, when there's plenty of sunlight and warmth, they should be moved slightly away from the window or protected using a sheer curtain.

NORTH: shade

A north-facing window offers the least light. Plants should be left in the window year-round. Choose robust plant species with dark green leaves, and other plants adapted to lower light levels. Consider splashing out on artificial lighting (see page 44) for your plants during the colder months.

Ferns cover the forest floor out in the wild, and so they prefer indirect light in a north-facing window. It may help to move them to an east-facing window during the three "death months".

Succulents love sunlight and prefer a south-facing window.

> **FACT**
>
> Plants that like lots of light need plenty of water – and plants that prefer shade need less water.

Which direction do your windows face? Here are few suggestions for what kind of plants could work in your home:

DIRECT SUNLIGHT: sun-worshippers

Plants such as aloe vera, spineless yucca (*Yucca elephantipes*) and cacti all love sunlight. They'll be happy with up to 6 hours of sunlight a day, so they'd love a spot in the sunniest place in your home.

INDIRECT LIGHT: shade-lovers

Most houseplants, such as Swiss cheese plants (*Monstera deliciosa*) and ferns, prefer partial shade. They're adapted to life on the forest floor, in the shade of big trees – and in your home, they would really like an environment that most closely resembles what they're used to out in the wild. They prefer some protection from the sun, so locate them near a window, or half behind a sheer curtain, where they will receive bright but diffused light.

SHADE: the basement-dwellers

A small minority of plants need so little light that they can cope in dark corners with low-light conditions. Emerald palm (*Zamioculcas zamiifolia*) and mother-in-law's tongue (*Sansevieria trifasciata*) do well in both poor and good light. What they can't cope with is too much water, as this rots their roots. You should therefore allow the soil in the pot to dry out completely between watering. The less light there is, the less water and food the plant needs.

HANDY HINT

Try imagining what your plants' natural habitats are like. Desert plants want conditions that are dry, warm and sunny. Tropical plants want moisture and warmth in partial shade, ideally with high ambient humidity.

It's not just humans who enjoy the summer. Plants really enjoy it as well – because they do most of their growing during the long, light summer days.

Grow lights – for healthy houseplants year-round

I can get a bit depressed during winter. My energy levels drop and tiredness creeps up on me. We're all affected by low light levels, and the same goes for plants. Their leaves become brittle, paler – the entire plant gets down in the mouth. Fortunately, there's a simple remedy that will banish your plants' winter blues: plant grow lights.

Isn't that cheating? No. Would you call it cheating to wash your clothes in a washing machine instead of by hand? We have the technology, and we can use it to create the best possible conditions for our plants. The new LED grow bulbs are also much more environmentally-friendly than the old-fashioned ones, and you can even use horticultural lighting to grow your own food throughout the winter – fresh herbs, for instance. Nothing tastes better than food that you've grown yourself!

So, if you want to create the best possible conditions for your plants, you can give them a real pick-me-up by using plant grow lighting during the colder months. You might be thinking this sounds complicated? Well it's not: grow bulbs and fluorescent tubes of various kinds are readily available from interiors shops and hardware stores. And they're not particularly expensive either.

You can use the bulbs in regular sockets. Screw in the bulb and place the light close to your plants. I generally place the light source half a metre (20in) away from the plant, whatever type of plant it is. Sun-loving plants do well close to plant lights, but those that prefer indirect light are happier situated slightly further away. Turn your plants now and again. Ideally, plants also need some time in the dark, so it's best to turn the light off at night.

You can use plant grow lights to improve growing conditions during the winter.

HANDY HINT

Switch on your plant light every morning before you leave your home – and switch it off again when you go to bed. It's even simpler if you buy a timer so that the plant light goes on and off automatically. Shops that sell plant grow lights usually sell timers as well. You should allow for about 16 hours of light a day. For my part, I've had good experience from using grow lights from October to March.

MIRRORS FOR INCREASING THE AMOUNT OF LIGHT

I also use mirrors to get extra light to my plants. The mirror reflects light onto the back of the plant, which helps it to thrive even more. This means that it's better able to tolerate being in a room with low light levels.

Mirrors improve lighting conditions and give you more flexibility in setting out your plants.

PRACTICAL ADVICE ABOUT WATERING

A lot of people I meet find the whole subject of watering plants a difficult one. Talking about it is always accompanied by a lot of sighing, as if they had a lot of plant deaths on their conscience. Watering isn't the easiest thing in the world, but nor is it the hardest. I think you'll manage – with the help of a few rules of thumb, although it's actually your finger that can save your plants.

Time to water? Here are two ways of finding out.

THE FINGER TRICK

Push your index finger a few centimetres into the potting compost. If it's dry when you bring it out and the compost falls away from your finger, you can water. If your finger is moist, and there is still some compost stuck to it when you pull it out, then there's still some water in the compost, so you don't need to water for about the next week.

WEIGH THE POT

If you're still not sure, lift up the pot. If it feels light, then there's not much water in it and you can water. If it feels heavy, then there's a lot of moisture in the compost and you can wait from a few days to a few weeks, depending on the type of plant.

FACTS

- The thicker the leaves, the less frequently you need to water.
- Most plants want to dry out between waterings.
- Water using water that's at room temperature.
- During the warmer months, most plants want to be watered at least once a week, but in the colder months you can cut right down to every two weeks or less. Always check the watering needs of individual plants – some are thirstier than others.
- Not enough water is better than too much – over-watering combined with low light levels is the number one cause of death for plants. Accidents are most common during the colder months.

Better not enough water than too much.

How much water does your plant want?

The thicker the leaves, the less often you need to water. Why is that? Plants with thick leaves – succulents, for instance – store water in their leaves because in their natural habitat they are accustomed to prolonged dry periods.

Plants with thin leaves need the opposite – more frequent watering and care – so succeeding with these plants is rather more challenging.

Make sure your pots have holes in the base, and ideally add a thin layer of leca balls or gravel in the bottom so that excess water can drain away. Most plants actually die from drowning rather than drying out. If plant roots are left standing in water, they rot and the plant dies. This is known as root rot.

If you buy a self-watering pot, you won't have to worry about the plant getting too much or too little water.

Water the entire pot so that the compost is thoroughly moistened. You'll then have to wait patiently until the compost is dry again.

Always check the plant's watering requirements, as these may vary substantially. Do a Google search if you need to!

WHY DO PLANTS DROOP WHEN THEY'RE DRY?

Plants draw water up from their roots. If the compost is dry, a plant won't get enough water to replace what it loses by evaporation from its leaves. The result is a drooping plant, and a sign that it needs water!

WATERING NEEDS THROUGHOUT THE YEAR
Spring light

Increasing amounts of light cause the plant to gradually need more water (one to two times a week).

Summer light

A lot of sunlight means that the plant needs a lot of water (one to three times a week).

Autumn light

As a result of shorter days, the plant gradually requires less water (one to four times a month).

Winter light

Not much light means that the plant needs only a little water (one to four times a month).

Some plants let you know when they need water. That's when they droop like this Chinese money plant, which is ready for watering.

WATERING DESERT PLANTS

Cacti and succulents like dry conditions, so they only need watering very occasionally. Give them a proper soaking to begin with, but then wait until they've completely dried out – you should probably leave a few weeks (perhaps even a few months) between watering. Desert plants need very little water during the winter, and just a bit more during the summer. Some succulents let you know when they need water – either their leaves wrinkle and shrivel up, or the leaves droop. If you can bear to be hard-hearted, wait until succulents really make it clear that they need water before watering.

WATERING TROPICAL PLANTS

Moisture-loving tropical plants, on the other hand – such as calathea, banana plants (*Musa*), bird of paradise plants (*Strelitzia*) and ferns – should be watered a few times a week, especially during the summer growing season. If they dry out, they will quickly die. Tropical potted plants enjoy warmth and moisture. If you're fortunate enough to have a bathroom with a window and underfloor heating, this will provide the ideal conditions. Constant moisture and steam from the shower, light from the bathroom window and heat from the floor will allow plants like this to thrive.

SHOULD I SPRAY MY PLANTS WITH WATER?

Yes, but the effect is the subject of much debate. Some people swear by giving their moisture-loving plants a daily mist to boost humidity, whereas others maintain it has no effect. I like to spray now and again, if only to remove some dirt and dust off their leaves.

Spraying or washing dust off the leaves has the following effects:

• The leaves breathe better.

• The leaves absorb more light, resulting in increased growth.

• The indoor air is improved.

• It makes it easier to combat spider mites, a pest that likes dry leaves.

My main argument for going around with a spray bottle is that it means I'm keeping an eye on my plants at the same time. And I can't help but believe that plants that are spoiled a bit will like me and reward me that bit more. When it comes to raising moisture levels, some people choose to use plant humidifiers, especially if they have a lot of tropical plants that like a humid environment.

Banana plant (*Musa*)

HANDY HINT

Using a soft, lukewarm cloth to wipe the leaves a few times in the year is even more effective than spraying to clean them. The ideal thing is to do both: spray first, then use a cloth to carefully dry the leaves.

Holiday watering

A lot of people ask what I do when I'm away from home. Who looks after my plants then? Here are six simple tips to help your plants survive while you're away on holiday.

Ask a friend The simplest approach is to ask another plant enthusiast to look after your plants. In my experience, there are a lot of people who like to look after other people's plants, and if you're away for a long time, you can of course foster them out for a while – or do like I do, and get someone to take up residence in your home while you're away.

Sun-screening Move your plants out of brightly sunlit windows into shade or half shade so that they need less water.

Wet newspaper Put some newspaper in the bottom of the sink or in a roasting tin, pour in plenty of water so that the newspaper soaks it up, and put your plants on top. They can now drink as much as they want. From experience, this method will keep your plants hydrated for up to two weeks. If you're away for longer, use a thicker layer of newspaper and drench accordingly.

The bottle trick Fill a large bottle with water, turn it upside down and push the open top into the compost. This also allows the plant to drink just as much as it needs. On average, this trick will water your plants for up to one week.

The bucket trick Fill a bucket with water and put it somewhere higher than the pots. Run lengths of thick twine from the bucket and down into the compost, using a pen to poke it down. Pack the compost around the twine, et voilà! You've made your own watering system. This method will keep your plants hydrated for up to two weeks. If you're away for longer, use a bigger bucket or container.

Self-watering pots These are an ingenious idea for when you're away travelling, because they make sure that your plants get exactly as much water as they need. On average, these will keep your plants hydrated for about a week or two, although different models may provide water for longer periods.

HANDY HINT

Potting compost can become hard and full of roots. As a result, the plant has difficulty absorbing water, which instead just runs through. When this happens, use a pen or a stick to dig around in the compost to create new "channels" for the water and for ventilation.

A large mineral water bottle filled with water and pushed upside down into the pot is a handy way to keep your plants hydrated while you're away.

Fiddle-leaf fig (*Ficus lyrata*)

PRACTICAL ADVICE ABOUT FEEDING

Plants need nutrition in order to grow and thrive. They get nutrients from the potting compost, but after a while, these start to run out as the plant "eats them up" and watering washes them away. That's why you need to add plant food.

A lot of people regard plant-feeding as advanced plant care, but it isn't. You can make it really complicated or else really simple. Me, I prefer simple. I feed indoor plants from March to September, and then from October to February I hardly do any feeding.

Plant food, or fertilizer, is available in many different forms: organic liquid plant food, artificial liquid plant food, fertilizer balls, fertilizer sticks, compost and so on. For my part, I swear by organic liquid plant food. I dilute it in water and my plants thrive on it. I prefer organic plant food to artificial plant food because it's more natural, environmentally friendly and sustainable.

Does plant-feeding sound complicated? Do you want to make feeding your plants as simple as possible? Get hold of some fertilizer balls or sticks. These are small balls that you spread on top of the potting compost a few times a year, or sticks that you poke down into the compost just as often. Both gradually release nutrients for your plants. Job done!

NO NEED TO COUNT YOUR CHICKENS

As a child, I grew up with free-range chickens in our garden. The result was a garden with the ideal level of nutrients. The regular application of chicken poop is like gunpowder for plants, providing them with plenty of nutrients. Because of the smell, you don't often find chicken poop being used on potted plants indoors, but there are plenty of other specialized plant food products you can use instead.

Organic plant food is my favourite.

Plant food from your own kitchen

Eggshells can be crushed and mixed into the potting compost. This gives your plants a calcium boost.

Banana peel can be cut up, dried and buried in the potting compost. Banana peel adds a lot of valuable minerals to the compost.

The water from boiling vegetables or eggs can be left to cool and given to plants, as it is rich in nutrients.

To make feeding as simple as possible, just scatter fertilizer balls in the top of the pot a few times a year. They usually last 3–6 months.

Feeding through the year

As a general rule, I feed my plants each week during the growing season, every 2 weeks beginning in autumn, and I stop feeding completely during the winter season, because that's when they're dormant and don't need as much feeding.

Here are my suggestions for feeding your plants throughout the year, based on Norway's seasons:

WINTER

You don't really need to apply any plant food during this period, but you can consider giving your plants a little bit of food now and again, say every two months – just for maintenance and up-keep. If you do, be thrifty and use a weak concentration.

SPRING

It is important to apply plant food in the spring – starting gradually as early as March, when the days are getting longer. One feed mid-March should be ample. In April you can step it up a little, with a feed about three weeks after the first – and then give your plants more in May, roughly every two weeks.

SUMMER

The plant is now at its best. It's enjoying the summer and, thanks to the light and the warmth, it's getting the maximum possible nutrition to grow big, strong and healthy. During the period from June to August you can apply a lot of plant food, but never more than recommended on the packaging!

AUTUMN

The plant is now getting ready for the winter, so we need to gradually cut back on feeding. You should therefore apply less and less food from September to October, approximately every two or three weeks.

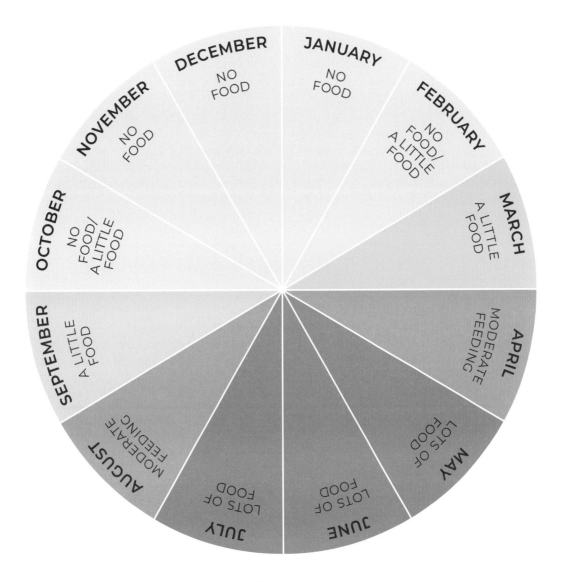

A timeline of feeding through the year, based on Nordic seasons.

PLANT CARE IN THE WINTER MONTHS

There's no getting away from it: looking after plants in a Nordic country is challenging, thanks to our long, dark winters. The main problem is the lack of natural light. In the depth of winter, we have darkness 18–19 hours a day. Even the UK, which is further south than Norway, is plunged into 16–17 hours of darkness on the shortest day.

It really is dispiriting to watch the fine, green plant that gave you so much joy in the warmer months as its leaves droop and turn yellow during the autumn, until it looks as if it's at death's door. "Just my luck", you think. "I'll never get it right."

We all have some plant deaths on our consciences. But don't give up – you just need to keep trying. I'm always doing it, and over time I've learnt a few new tricks that have helped me prevent more and more plants from saying their goodbyes. It's a lot to do with access to light. If you can crack the light + water code, then there's a good chance that you'll succeed. The main rule is: the more light there is, the more water. At the same time, we must never forget that plants are all different, so they have different needs.

Maybe you think everything looks so easy and simple on my Instagram account? But believe me, I've sent lots of plants straight to their graves. In particular, a lot of desert plants have suffered death from drowning because, in my eagerness to water, I've overwhelmed them with both water and plant food during the winter season. Even though this was done with the best of intentions, they abruptly turned yellow and then lost all their leaves. I have been annoyed by many a plant – but I have also known the joy of a plant suddenly perking up and displaying a continued desire to live.

DRY INDOOR AIR KILLS

A lot of plants are killed off during the winter by dry indoor air. A lot of newly built properties have really poor air flow that creates problem conditions for plants. Radiators are also a threat, so if you really want to create a good indoor climate, get yourself a humidifier and keep your plants away from radiators. Humidifiers are available in various sizes, and they produce a tropical effect that will do wonders for your little green oasis.

Winter care

Plants are like us humans during the winter: more tired and with less vitality. How can you best protect them during what I call the three "death months"?

Simple winter care tips

• Put plants near a window to ensure they get as much daylight as possible.

• Give less water. Plants are dormant at this time of year and need much less water.

• Stop or reduce feeding.

• Turn each plant every week to distribute the available light over all the leaves.

• Don't leave them close to a radiator – keep them away from heat sources.

Tips for the more advanced grower

• Additional full-spectrum artificial lighting can be a good idea.

• Avoid cold draughts from open windows – cold air stresses plants and can cause them to wilt.

• Wipe the leaves with a damp cloth – dust on the leaves prevents the plant from absorbing light.

• Showering or misting will provide moisture for the leaves in dry winter air.

IS A PLANT DEAD IF IT'S LOSING LEAVES?

No, not necessarily. But if it has lost its leaves due to a combination of lack of light and too much water, there is a risk of it getting root rot. This is when the roots drown from being left standing in water, causing them to rot. So what can you do about root rot?

• Move the plant to the sunniest spot in your home and leave it to dry out before watering it again.

• Remove any dead or yellow leaves.

• If the potting compost is soaking wet and you have underfloor heating, put the pot on the warm floor for a few days to allow the compost to dry out a bit.

If you're in luck, the plant will put out fresh green leaves after a few weeks. Seeing your plant come back from the dead like that is a really good feeling! However, don't forget that some plants become dormant in winter. Figs, kiwis and ginkgos, for example, are supposed to drop their leaves at this time. If one of your plants has dropped its leaves, it might have just gone into hibernation and is waiting for spring to come around.

Some plants, like this fig, have a life cycle of going into hibernation for a while and dropping their leaves, before putting out fresh, new shoots and leaves in the spring.

PLANT CARE IN THE SUMMER MONTHS

Summers in northern Europe offer pleasant temperatures and long, light days, which are perfect for most plants. Their needs in the summer are much the same as ours: hydration and keeping out of strong sunlight. Without protection of some kind, most plant species will get sunburnt.

Who hasn't overdone it after the long winter months and ended up with sunburn? When a plant gets sunburn, it can be weeks before the damage becomes visible in the form of brown and yellowish patches on the leaves. Don't despair though, because the plant usually puts out new leaves, though it may take a few weeks.

Your plants need to acclimatize to sunlight. So, if you want to move plants you've overwintered in a dark corner of your home out onto the balcony, they'll need some time to get used to the new conditions. And give them just a little water now and again. (See page 65 for more information.)

The same principle applies indoors. If you're moving plants from a fairly dark corner to a window in full sunlight, start by leaving them in half shade near the window for two weeks, before putting them directly in the window. If you do put plants in the window, you can use a sheer curtain to provide some half shade.

HANDY HINT

Are you unsure whether a windowsill might be too hot for your plants in the summer? Try putting your hand on the window in the middle of the day. If it feels too hot for you, then it will be too hot for your plants as well.

Summer care indoors

• Avoid sun damage by putting your plant to one side of the window or behind a sheer curtain.

• Remember to increase light gradually when moving a plant into a bright window.

• The more light and warmth your plant gets, the more water it needs.

• If it's raining, you could put your plant out for an hour to rinse off any dust.

• Plants grow during the summer and they need nutrients, so increase the amount of fertilizer.

Since there is more light during the warmer months, you can put your plants in places where they would not do well during the winter, such as in a north-facing window or further into the room.

Putting plants outdoors

If you're lucky enough to have a balcony or a garden, you can move your houseplants outside during the warmer months.

BENEFITS
• Plants love the light – and there's much more light outdoors, so your plant will grow more quickly.

• Your outdoor space will be lush and green and this will free up space indoors.

• Thanks to the ideal light conditions, some plants that are normally shy to flower may put on a show when they are in peak condition.

DRAWBACKS
• The transition to outdoors can be tricky. You have to take account of wind, rain and temperature drops. Plants drink much more water outdoors, so they'll need more frequent watering and looking after – especially if it doesn't rain.

• Plants also need more plant food outdoors because of the improved growing conditions.

WHAT YOU SHOULD DO?
• Put your plant outside when the night-time temperature doesn't fall below 10°C (50°F). Leave it in full shade for two weeks, then take one to two weeks to gradually acclimatize it to sunlight (in half shade).

• Overcast weather is perfect as full sunlight can burn the leaves.

• If leaves become scorched (you can tell by brown and yellow patches on the leaves after one week), don't despair. Just trim away the damaged leaves and the plant will most likely put out new leaves after a little while.

DON'T FORGET

• A houseplant needs to be robust for outdoor summer living, so check to see whether your plant can cope with the elements before putting it outside.

• Don't use a pot outdoors without drainage holes! Rainwater will drown your plant, so make sure the pot has drainage holes.

• Plants drink more the more sunlight they get, so water more during dry periods.

• Wind dries out soil faster.

• Cacti and succulents can stand in full sunlight, but perhaps bring them under cover when there is lots of rain in order to prevent death by drowning.

• Tropical plants prefer half shade and will quickly burn in full sunlight.

A lot of houseplants can benefit from being outdoors during the summer, like this tropical white bird of paradise (*Strelitzia nicolai*).

POTS

POTS MADE FROM BREATHABLE NATURAL MATERIALS

Most plants prefer to be in pots made from breathable natural materials, such as unglazed terracotta. Many plant pots are made from clay. Unglazed clay is porous, which allows air to pass through into the soil and to the plant's roots, which is good for most plants. However, the downside is that moisture evaporates quickly from the soil. As a result, unglazed clay pots are particularly good for plants that don't mind drying out, such as succulents and cacti.

What's the white coating that you often get on clay pots? This is caused by mineral salts seeping through the pot. I think clay pots with different colours and shades are decorative – but then I like the rustic look.

PLASTIC POTS FOR PLANTS THAT LIKE WET COMPOST

If you have a plant that likes constantly damp compost, you can go for a plastic pot, because they're better at retaining moisture. Both ferns and papyrus (*Cyperus papyrus*) grow well in damp conditions, so they'll do well in plastic pots. Pots with glazing on the outside are also watertight, so they're also good at retaining moisture.

CHOOSING A POT SIZE FOR YOUR PLANT

The smaller the pot, the quicker the soil will dry out; the bigger the pot, the longer the soil will stay damp. You should therefore choose the right pot for the size of your plant:

• A big pot with a small plant can result in over-watering – causing the roots to drown and rot.

• A big plant in a small pot can lead to drying out – the roots can't get enough water and nutrients from the soil.

Both papyrus (*Cyperus papyrus*) (left) and ferns (top right) like damp conditions and will do well in plastic pots.

COMPOST AND REPOTTING

You should repot your plants roughly every year or every other year. You can choose either to repot your plant into a new and bigger pot, or to replace the soil in the existing pot. The best time for repotting is in spring.

For my part, I'm not that organized and I make a lot of mess with soil, so I try to do my repotting outdoors – or else I put bin bags down on the floor before I get started. You will need a new pot, potting compost and leca balls or gravel.

1 Give your plant a good soaking before you begin.

2 Carefully pull the plant out of its existing pot, making sure that the rootball comes with it.

3 Carefully remove some of the soil from around the rootball.

4 Put some leca or gravel into the bottom of the new pot, followed by a little potting compost.

5 Place the plant in the centre of the pot. The top of the rootball needs to sit about 2.5cm (1in) below the rim of the pot, so adjust the compost in the base accordingly.

6 Fill the space around the plant with compost, adding some to the top.

7 Carefully pack the compost around the plant so that the top roots are covered.

8 Give the plant another good soaking. Voilà! That's it.

HANDY HINT

It's best to repot newly purchased plants
straight away so that they get a good start.
Most plants are grown in greenhouses so that
they look as good as possible when they are in
the shop, and as a result they're usually too big
for their pot. When repotting a plant, choose
a pot with a diameter that's a few centimetres
(1–2in) larger.

If the plant has a strong rootball and you want
to keep it in its current pot – meaning that you
only want to replace the soil – you can prune
away some of the larger roots when you repot it.

Always use new, nutrient-rich compost to give
plants a good start. Previously used compost
is low in nutrients and can also contain pests
and diseases. After a few weeks or months,
when the plant is growing well, you can add
a little plant food.

PLANT GROOMING

How do you know when your plants are doing fine?
Check the leaves. The condition of the leaves is a good
indicator of the plant's health. Healthy, happy plants have
naturally strong, green leaves.

But what happens when the leaves don't look healthy? It's never easy to give a simple answer here. The reason is usually so complex that it can easily end in frustration. Here are a few tips, based on my own experience.

The leaves are curling up and shrivelling
Not enough water. If the leaves are shrivelling, drooping and look wrinkled, this is a sign that your plant needs to fill its cells with water. For a long drink, put the pot in a filled sink or in a bucket and allow the plant to soak up water. After a few hours you'll see the plant perking up again as the cells in the leaves and stem fill with water.

The leaves have brown patches Sun damage, dry indoor air, lack of nutrients, not enough water, pests. Cut away the damaged and brown leaves. After a few weeks, your plant will usually put out new leaves. If it's winter, spray the plant with water and wipe the leaves with a damp cloth. This will remove any dust and add moisture to the leaves. Dry indoor air is a common cause of leaves drying out and producing brown patches.

Try carefully rinsing the plant with lukewarm water in the shower.

The leaves are becoming pale or turning light green Lack of nutrients. If the plant is losing its colour, it may need more plant food. Perhaps there aren't enough nutrients left in the soil, in which case the options are feeding or repotting. Most plants also need plenty of light. Move the plant to a brighter place, such as on a windowsill. If the plant isn't getting enough light and if you have also over-fed it, cut out or reduce the amount of fertilizer you give it.

The leaves are turning yellow Root rot from too much water, not enough light, too much plant food, pests. Yellow leaves are the surest sign of an unwell plant. The most common cause is over-watering, which leads to root rot. If the soil is waterlogged, cut back on the watering and allow the soil to dry out thoroughly. Remove any yellow leaves.

There are small black spots, a coating or white patches Insects and pests (see pages 74–5).

INSECTS AND PESTS

Insects on potted plants are not nice – or rather, they're creepy. I've actually had them visiting and they cause me a lot of anxiety. Fortunately, there are a lot of folk remedies for getting the better of pests and insects. I've found over 100 of them while researching for this book – though some could be described as better substantiated than others. The advice about putting your plant in the microwave to get rid of aphids is not something I'd set much store by!

THE FRUIT FLY TRAP

You will need: a glass, water, vinegar and washing-up liquid.

1. Half-fill the glass with vinegar (about 100ml/3fl oz), and top up with water (about 100ml/3fl oz) so that you have a 50/50 mixture of vinegar and water. Add one drop of washing-up liquid.

2. Place the glass near to the pot you suspect of harbouring fruit flies/fungus gnats. The bigger the problem, the more traps you can put out.

3. The fruit flies/fungus gnats will seek out the mixture (they are attracted to the scent of vinegar), land on the top of it, become trapped and sink to the bottom of the glass.

I often leave a fruit-fly trap out during the warmer months, just behind the plant pots. It regularly catches any fruit flies or fungus gnats that are about – and as soon as the mixture has evaporated, I fill it up again.

Don't forget that you only need to use pesticides when the plant is suffering from a bad attack. Check plants in the shop before taking them home: if you buy healthy plants and look after them well, then in theory you should be able to avoid both insect attacks and disease. There's a vast range of different pests, but I'll just concentrate on some of the most common ones that affect potted plants – as well as some effective ways of getting rid of them.

FRUIT FLIES

The most important measure is to make sure that your houseplants are not too wet. If you get an infestation, allow the soil to dry out thoroughly. Yellow glue traps can help. My best tip is the fruit fly trap. This is a simple, environmentally friendly and effective way of getting rid of fruit flies, though it's also effective against the notorious little fungus gnats that often pop up in the summer – especially in homes where bananas and other types of fruit or food leftovers are left out.

APHIDS, MILDEW AND SPIDER MITES

Make your own environmentally friendly insecticide from cooking oil and a mild liquid soap. The oil forms a suffocating coating on aphids, mites and eggs, while the soap dries them out.

Mix 2 tablespoons of vegetable oil, 3 tablespoons of liquid soap and 250ml (8fl oz) of water in a spray bottle and spray over the entire plant.

If it's a really bad attack, repeat after 1–2 weeks. It's a good idea to test the mixture on just one leaf at first, just to make sure that your plant can tolerate it.

LIQUID SOAP AGAINST PESTS

Some people swear by liquid soap and have achieved good results washing their pest-stricken plants with a diluted mild liquid soap. There are two methods to choose from:

The bucket method

Fill a large bucket with water and add about a dessertspoon of a mild liquid soap. Stir in well. Turn the plant upside-down and slowly dip the plant up and down in the bucket. Afterwards, rinse the plant using clean lukewarm water, ideally in the shower. Only the green parts of the plant and the stem need to be immersed – not the soil in the pot.

The massage method

Carefully wash and massage the leaves and the stem in diluted mild liquid soap as above, remembering to wash particularly carefully underneath the leaves all the way to the stem.

CAN CLEAN, LUKEWARM WATER HELP AGAINST PESTS?

Yes, it is worth testing this simple method. Myself, I've found that washing plants in the shower or in the basin using clean, lukewarm water works well. Thoroughly washing the leaves – on top and underneath, as well as the stalks – will often be enough to get rid of these pests. I've also found that it helps to carefully massage leaves with my fingers to ensure that insects, spider mites etc. are washed off.

POISON – WHEN ALL ELSE FAILS

I have been forced to resort to chemicals, albeit very rarely. This should be avoided if possible, but if you have a plant that is particularly valuable or big and which is that bit special to you, you can use an insecticide. I decided to get hold of a chemical aphid spray when my 2m (6½ft) orange tree was attacked by aphids – and it worked. However, I do try to limit my use of chemicals to situations where my entire plant collection is at risk. If you get mealy bugs, you can try removing them using cotton buds dipped in methylated spirit. Unfortunately, it's really difficult to get rid of this much-feared bug, and you have to consider throwing the plant out to prevent it infecting other plants. Better luck next time!

STYLING AND DECORATING WITH PLANTS

Nordic interior design is so pure, airy, light and simple that rooms can benefit from a few plants. Green elements in an otherwise austere interior create depth and contrast. Interior magazines feature articles on the sort of lush, green homes you'd like to walk into and stay for a while. Not surprisingly, plants have become an integral part of our interior spaces, in the same way as cushions, textiles and curtains – but with the added bonus that they bring life into the home.

YOUR OWN GREEN OASIS

Every time I walk into a lush, green home, I always think: the person who lives here is able to show that they care, both for people and for all other living things. Plants can make any home feel more personal and full of life – all it takes is some awareness of placing.

THE TRINITY

All good things come in threes, and that also applies to arranging plants. Try placing them in groups of three – for harmony, structure and interest. Put a larger plant at the back, a medium-sized one to one side and a smaller one at the front, in a triangular arrangement. It's a grouping that can also include more than three plants at a time, but note that odd numbers usually work better than even numbers in combinations of this kind. You could also try experimenting with combinations of different greens and leaf textures to create a more vivid impression.

PLANTS ON THE TABLE – A SUSTAINABLE ALTERNATIVE

I like arranging several low-growing plants on a dish and putting it on my coffee table or dining table. At the risk of killing the romance for rose lovers, I do think plants are a more sustainable alternative to always having fresh-cut flowers in a vase. Both cacti and succulents can work just as well as attention-grabbers on the table, ideally in a small arrangement. You can also make a simple terrarium by putting plants inside a glass container.

HOUSEPLANTS AS NET CURTAINS

If you live in a densely populated area with neighbours opposite, plants can help to preserve your privacy. Place plants in and next to windows to create a green and smooth transition between indoor and outdoor spaces – while also ensuring that fewer people can see in.

PLANTS AS ROOM DIVIDERS

My partner's flat is one big open space from the entrance through to the kitchen and living-room. In order to create distinct zones, he uses plants as dividers and to mark out areas. Larger plants work fine as room dividers – they can form a sort of half-hedge to create a room within a larger space. If your plants are not so tall, try putting them on pedestals or occasional tables to achieve much the same effect.

A big Swiss cheese plant (*Monstera deliciosa*) works well as a room divider.

THE PLANT NOOK

In big, open spaces, it can be really nice to have a green plant nook. My partner Erik has created a peaceful oasis in his apartment by surrounding a corner chair with plants. Try it yourself, by putting a large green plant (or more) in a corner, perhaps next to a seat.

Maybe you have a low bench or an occasional table? You could place these next to the chair and arrange different-size plants on them at varying heights. Try some on the floor as well. If you turn your head, it can almost be like sitting out in a garden as your plants catch your gaze.

A green setting is the ideal place to sit and read a book or to contemplate. An extra benefit of putting plants near where you sit is that it's easier to see when they need watering.

PLANTS HANGING HIGH UP

Hanging plants are possibly my favourites, and they can give any room a lift. Ivy (*Hedera*), waxplant (*Hoya*), golden pothos (*Epipremnum aureum*) and string of pearls (*Curio rowleyanus*, formerly known as *Senecio rowleyanus*) will all really benefit from being raised up in a hanging plant pot. They have trailing branches that make them ideal for suspending from the ceiling or in front of a window, for instance.

These days there are a lot of excellent pot-hangers available in various materials – macramé, basketwork, metal, ceramic. In my experience, I think it creates a more lively and harmonic impression to arrange several hanging plant pots in a row, of various sizes and at different heights. In smaller spaces and homes, you can free up valuable floor space by hanging plants.

THE WOW FACTOR

One single, large and luxuriantly green plant can be an eye-catcher in any room. A tree of a certain size, such as a big fiddle-leaf fig (*Ficus lyrata*), a robust Swiss cheese plant (*Monstera deliciosa*) or an over-sized bird of paradise plant (*Strelitzia*), is guaranteed to give the space the attention it deserves, whether it's a large room or a spacious entrance hall.

Note: these are plants that take time to grow big, or cost a lot to buy as a mature specimen – so patience or a generous wallet (or piggy bank) may be useful resources.

 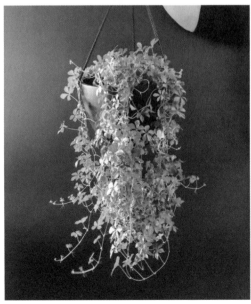

Large plants, such as an elegant olive tree, in your living-room make a natural focal point.

PLANT SHELVES

One or more plant shelves in your kitchen and living-room will instantly give your home a green and lush impression. You can find inspiration on Instagram by searching for the hashtag #plantshelfie.

In the kitchen, I like to combine edible and decorative houseplants. I enjoy having access to herbs that I use a lot in dishes, such as parsley, basil, coriander and thyme. I find that having these herbs close to hand makes me use them more. Herbs smell good – and they provide inspiration in my cooking.

Use your plant shelf to highlight items that you're particularly fond of. I have my collection of hand-glazed ceramic animals – they're a bit kitsch, but kind of fun to have among the green plants.

WALL PLANTS

Try buying pots that can be fastened to vertical surfaces, so that you can hang plants from the wall. Some ferns work really well here – and if you want to be particularly creative, you could try using different hanging plants to create a green wall.

Golden pothos (*Epipremnum aureum*) is a good candidate.

Moss walls are commercially available in various sizes. These can be hung directly on the wall and are practically maintenance-free. I've also seen cactus walls – mixed, live cacti arranged in an exciting vertical display. In Barcelona, I saw an original cactus wall containing over 100 types to form a striking tapestry of silvery greens.

BRIGHTEN UP UNUSED CORNERS

Every home has an unused nook that has never really fitted in. But as long as it has some access to natural light, one or more plants can transform a neglected corner into something more interesting and alive. And if there's no natural light available, you can always get a plant light.

Sunny, warm corners are perfect for sun-loving plants such as cacti and succulents. How about a sunny corner with a desert feel as a contrasting feature to lusher plants elsewhere?

An arrangement of houseplants can brighten up any corner.

MIRRORS – MY FAVOURITE TIP

I have twice as many plants as I really have! Or at least, that's how it looks – in my mirrors. An ingenious trick then is to use mirrors as part of your interior décor – especially if, like me, you live in a small space. Mirrors reflect light further into a room and make the space feel bigger. In particular, because they increase the amount of natural light, mirrors allow you to place plants further in from windows.

Mirrors of different shapes and sizes also help to create interesting dynamics in an interior space. I have a lot of mirrors of all shapes: square, rounded, completely round, and in various sizes as well.

POTS AND JARS

People often ask me where I get my pots. I tell them that I like to combine everything imaginable – new and secondhand, home-made and non-traditional containers, pots and jars. Check to see what you already have in your cupboards and storage spaces. Perhaps you'll find an unused bowl that you can use as a pot holder?

I usually reuse these by drilling a hole in the bottom for drainage. You can easily do this yourself by sticking a piece of gaffer tape on the bottom and then carefully drilling a hole through it. A lot of towns and cities have shops run by charitable foundations and organizations that sell secondhand and recycled items. It can be exciting to go on a treasure hunt while contributing to sustainable recycling and a good cause at the same time.

POTS FROM SECONDHAND MARKETS

Local flea markets or neighbourhood car boot sales are other potential sources of treasures. Maybe you'll find an old tin that would make a good container for some of your succulents? Or a rattan basket that could be lined with plastic and used as an attractive pot container? There are plenty of opportunities if you have a creative and imaginative vision – you'll get a lot for your money and it's good for the environment. When I'm away travelling, I like to visit markets and vintage stores. I often make impulse purchases that go on to bring me immense joy – and that are all mine! An old, green glass bowl from Burgundy, France, has served as a pot for one of my ferns, and an old wooden measuring jug that we found at a market in Portugal is doing a splendid job as a pot holder for a climbing plant. They now sit there as constant reminders of the great times we had on those trips.

Two miniature cacti planted in old water glasses. If you can manage to drill holes in the small bases, they work well as pots.

How can you double the number of plants in your room? Get a mirror!

DARK WALLS MAKE YOUR PLANTS REALLY STAND OUT

A lot of people are scared that dark walls will make the room
look gloomy, but my experience is the direct opposite – they
create a warm atmosphere, and they work as a bold canvas
that makes your plants stand out. Dark shades of grey, green
and blue on a wall will only enhance the colour of the leaves
and give depth to your green oasis.

Dark walls and vibrant, green
leaves are a perfect combination.

TABLES, PEDESTALS AND STOOLS

Variation is the keyword. I consciously made use of a lot of
different elements when I furnished my home with plants.
I grouped several plants on small tables, put plants both
on and underneath pedestals, or used unused stools to elevate
and accentuate my plants. I think plants arranged at different
heights look great. Getting them up off the floor and putting
them on stools or occasional tables creates an airy, luxuriant
and delicate impression.

A pedestal suggestion that's a bit out of the ordinary – turn
large unused jars upside-down and use them as stands for
potted plants.

Try raising your plants up on
pedestals or jars for an airy feel.

GREEN IDEAS FOR A MORE LUXURIANT HOME

Current interior trends are clearly characterized by natural and organic features.

As well as houseplants, there's a whole lot of cool poster art that can bring a natural element into a room, with attractive, clean foliage motifs. How about hanging a nice picture of a lush monstera over the sofa?

The natural theme can be complemented by textiles in plant prints. An attractive cushion with a leaf motif can brighten up any armchair or sofa – and elegant wallpaper patterns can be used to enhance a luxuriant, tropical mood. A rear wall that gets very little daylight papered with a botanical design will definitely give the room an organic feel.

The more original your idea for accentuating your plants, the better it usually works. Try out some ideas to see what looks good!

PLANTS ROOM BY ROOM

Upgrading your home with plants to create a more distinctive and personal interior is relatively cheap and rewarding. While the decision of what plants work well in what location is, in many ways, a matter of taste, it's also possible to take a more scientific approach to the positioning of plants within the home. Join me on a tour of the different rooms in the house to find inspiration and get ideas!

The hallway

The hallway is the space that creates the first impression of a home, so it's bound to influence the overall experience. I've recently been spending some time in Portugal – for work and study – and over there in Europe's western outpost, they have a tradition of filling the hallway with plants in order to welcome guests. That's a tradition I can get behind!

The hallway has both a practical and an aesthetic function. This is where outdoor clothing and shoes belong, while at the same time inviting you into the rest of the house. To my mind, hanging pots are always ideal for hallways. That way you make the most of the available height while freeing up valuable floor space. Maybe try a golden pothos (*Epipremnum aureum*), an ivy (*Hedera*) or a waxplant (*Hoya*). These are plants that can tolerate a little neglect and low light levels and put up with a draught from an open front door.

Houseplants in the hallway provide a welcome for guests.

The living-room

This is the room for relaxation, recreation and activities. The living-room can provide space for plenty of plants, but it can be nice to have one eye-catching plant – and for that, a tree is ideal. A large fiddle-leaf fig (*Ficus lyrata*), a tropical banana plant (*Musa*) or an extravagant bird of paradise plant (*Strelitzia*) is guaranteed to give your room a lift and create an elegant impression.

The living-room allows you to think big. It's usually the largest room in the home, so we have a bit more space in which to overindulge. It generally has a few windows that let in light, which is important for plants to grow and thrive. Here a plant can be like a piece of furniture in itself and generally enhances the interior. Other plant types that look good in the living-room are areca palms (*Dypsis lutescens*), ferns, paperplants (*Fatsia japonica*) and rubber plants (*Ficus elastica*). Treat yourself to a big prima donna in the living-room, one that can just stand there and draw attention to itself. How about a big Swiss cheese plant (*Monstera deliciosa*)?

Plants in the living-room also create atmosphere, dampen noise and work really well as screens and room dividers. In my own living-room, I've got rid of both the TV and a whole lot of surplus furniture in order to make room for more plants.

The living-room is the ideal space for creating your own green oasis.

The kitchen

The kitchen is the beating heart of most homes. This is where we get together for meals and conversation, and often there's a windowsill or a shelf full of herbs. For my part, I like to have the herbs that I use most in cooking, such as parsley, basil, coriander, thyme and oregano, close to hand. You can buy small worktop propagators with built-in plant grow lights that provide ideal growing conditions through the dark winter months. You can also use plant grow lights for your own greens, such as lettuce, sprouts and radishes, year-round.

Citrus bushes and trees belong in the kitchen. Calamondin (*Citrus* x *microcarpa*) and lemon (*Citrus limon*) can easily find their way into your food, and when I'm making myself a gin and tonic at the weekend, there's always a slice in it.

The small calamondins from the tree are really sour, but the fun of having grown them myself is definitely sweet!

I also have a coffee plant (*Coffea arabica*) on my worktop. It has decorative, shiny leaves, and perhaps in a few years it will grow into a small tree – and maybe even produce enough coffee beans to give me a low-food miles espresso ... I can dream, can't I?

A separate plant shelf is a practical and attractive addition to any kitchen. Fill it with a selection of herbs and decorative plants, and a handful of good cookery books and a few knick-knacks that you're fond of.

Calamondin (*Citrus* x *microcarpa*) is a robust citrus plant that copes well indoors in most homes. The tart fruit can be used in cooking as a replacement for lemon or lime.

Coffee plant (*Coffea arabica*)

The bedroom

Everyone enjoys a good night's sleep. That's why it's so important to have a bedroom that creates the best possible conditions for rest. A lot of people are sceptical about having plants in the bedroom, but there's no reason to be. Healthy, living plants are good for indoor air – unlike dying plants, which reduce air quality.

In fact, there are plants that are particularly suitable for the bedroom because they produce oxygen at night. Better still, they remove toxic substances (volatile organic compounds/VOCs), such as trichloroethylene and formaldehyde, from the air while you sleep. They do this by absorbing the toxins through their leaves and into their roots where the VOCs are neutralized and converted into plant food. This combination is ideal for creating an indoor climate in which to sleep – plants cleaning the air and producing oxygen at the same time!

A particularly good choice here is mother-in-law's tongue (*Sansevieria trifasciata*) and aloe vera. These are plants that are fairly resistant to temperature fluctuations, which are quite common in bedrooms (with airing and open windows at night). Another good alternative is lavender (*Lavandula*), even if it isn't exactly a houseplant. Lavender gives off a pleasant and subdued scent known for its calming effect, while at the same time it's one of the easiest garden plants to grow indoors, as long as it gets plenty of sunlight.

The bathroom

The bathroom can be a challenging environment for plants – often with little or no access to daylight. But if you're lucky enough to have a window in your bathroom, then you'll have ideal growing conditions.

Regular showers and water vapour create a climate in which ferns, a number of tropical plants and other moisture-loving plants can thrive. This is because they're used to rainforest conditions – and in a light and humid bathroom, a banana plant (*Musa*), a calathea or a climbing Swiss cheese plant (*Monstera deliciosa*) are all good options.

If you don't have any daylight in your bathroom, succulents can cope for a few weeks at a time before being moved close to a window. I have a handful of emerald palms (*Zamioculcas zamiifolia*) standing in the middle of my bathroom without access to daylight, and these cope fine with the combination of light from the ceiling spotlights and the moisture in the air.

If you don't have a window in your bathroom, you can always invest in a plant grow light, which will allow you to create a green oasis there (see page 44).

You can also add a bit of greenery to your bathroom with a vase containing a leaf cut from a Swiss cheese plant, a flower stem from an orchid or a twig from a pruned olive tree.

Garage, loft and basement

These are perfect places for some plants to overwinter after spending the summer outdoors. Once the temperature starts falling in the autumn – before the night-time frosts set in – you need to move olive trees, citrus trees and palms inside. These plants are accustomed to a Mediterranean climate, so it's important to recreate the climate that they normally have during the winter. They then do best if they get to be semi-dormant, at temperatures between 0°C and 10°C (32°F and 50°F), with some light and just a little water once a month.

Other houseplants in pots that can overwinter frost-free in the garage, loft or basement are ivy (*Hedera*), fig (*Ficus carica*) and ginkgo.

The home office

When you're studying or working at home, it can be inspiring to allow your eyes to rest on an interesting plant with attractive foliage. My own office favourites are variants of calathea or a colourful begonia. If you're often away from the office, you should choose a plant that doesn't mind drying out, such as an emerald palm (*Zamioculcas zamiifolia*) or various kinds of succulents or cacti.

Houseplants don't just improve your working environment aesthetically – numerous studies have shown that their calming, green presence also boosts productivity.

ENJOYING GREENERY IN THE WORKPLACE

The question of what plants might fit best in a workplace depends on the people who work there. If you have at least a few green enthusiasts among your colleagues, it should be possible to have a lot of plants – and maybe even very high-maintenance ones.

But if you're the kind of person who waters office plants with coffee dregs (something that actually helps to kill them), you should go for plants with thick, green leaves that can tolerate drying out between waterings. Good choices – which are also known to clean indoor air of chemical toxins – are golden pothos (*Epipremnum aureum*), mother-in-law's tongue (*Sansevieria trifasciata*) and areca palm (*Dypsis lutescens*).

THE GREEN HOME IN PRACTICE

All over the world, air quality is getting worse – and especially in the big cities. As a result, air pollution in our homes is also increasing, but in Oslo, where I live, the city council has managed to buck this trend in the last few years – by investing in public transport and pedestrianizing streets where people can move about in green surroundings. Yet despite the city's best efforts, the air in Oslo is still harmful and there's more to be done. Those of us who live in towns and cities can do our bit for public health by keeping houseplants in our homes and maybe even a plant or two in the workplace because, in spite of everything, many of us spend about 90 per cent of our time indoors.

The benefits of bringing nature indoors

Have you heard of the concepts nature-deficit disorder (NDD) and the forest air effect? NDD refers to the idea that many people, and especialy children, suffer from not spending enough time outdoors. This lack of contact with nature in our lives, and living in environments characterized by stress, noise and sitting down, can cause numerous physical and mental problems. In Norway, researchers at the University of Life Sciences have identified a solution they call the forest air effect: bringing nature indoors. They discovered that by introducing green indoor plants into the home and workplace, people experience a greater sense of calm, presence and contentment. They feel more confident and less tired – the so-called forest air effect.

Another concern is air pollution. According to the World Health Organization (WHO), air pollution causes the deaths of seven million people every year. That's scary reading! Sources of air pollution include motor vehicles, industry, cattle farming and coal-powered electricity generation. Deforestation is making the problem worse and a large number of plants and trees are disappearing as ever-greater quantities of toxins are emitted. The result is that the air we breathe is far from clean. In the Indian city of New Delhi, the air was (and still is) so polluted that in 1992 the researcher and environmental campaigner Kamal Meattle suffered from allergic reactions that nearly killed him. His lung capacity at the time had been reduced to 70 per cent. Kamal could see that something had to be done – both for himself and for everyone else in New Delhi. He had studies conducted that showed how effective houseplants were at influencing our working environment, both mentally and physically.

Based on the research available from the National Aeronautics and Space Administration (NASA) and other bodies, including the Institution of Engineering and Technology (IET), Kamal found that there are three really common houseplants that have a proven ability to help improve the indoor climate: golden pothos (*Epipremnum aureum*), mother-in-law's tongue (*Sansevieria trifasciata*) and areca palm (*Dypsis lutescens*). In a widely viewed TED Talk, he calmly explains how we can all use common houseplants that are easy to find in plant shops to "refresh" our interior environments.

Kamal tried out these plants in the building where he himself worked. The research established that employees were at less risk of headache, reduced lung capacity, asthma and other symptoms. Productivity also increased by 20 per cent.

HANDY HINT

By putting several plants together, you are creating a tiny forest. In this miniature forest, the plants start a collaboration project in which they all breathe together, release moisture and at the same time remove harmful substances from your indoor air. Not only is this forest beautiful, it is working to improve your health and well-being.

FACT

All plants convert carbon dioxide to oxygen, though not all plants have air-cleaning capabilities. According to NASA, air-cleaning plants are characterized by the fact that they remove VOCs from the air. Plants that are particularly good at cleaning air are mainly from tropical and subtropical regions.

The healing power of plants for mental health

In my daytime job, I work as a therapist. It's a job that entails both uplifting and difficult conversations with patients, many of whom have been exposed to traumatic events. I love my job – it gives my day meaning. But listening to people's pain also takes it out of me. For me, coming home after work and pushing my fingers down into potting compost is good specialist therapy. I wind down, shift focus and am aware of my breathing calming down. I believe that plants have a healing effect on us. Plants are also a form of therapy that is readily available to all of us – and which we all can afford.

I also have 20 plants at my office. I don't believe that the plants on the windowsill in my workplace are unimportant. They listen patiently and then get on with their business. Research supports the idea that the presence of plants alone can soothe bad feelings. It's not surprising, then, that so many people turn to tending plants when their heads are full of frustration and worry. Plants can help to alleviate emotional pain and shift focus onto life and growth. They do say that the colour of hope is green.

MORE PLANTS MEAN LESS TIME OFF SICK

At Google's Norwegian office, they have brought the natural world inside, created a rainforest-like atmosphere and installed plant grow lights in order to provide good growing conditions for their many plants. Google Norway has a rate of absence due to illness of less than one per cent – which is interesting, because nationally the rate is over six per cent. The director of Google Norway, Jan Grønbech, points to the correlation between surroundings and sick leave, and suggests that the cause might be the attractive and organic environment.

At Google, the results are evident in the fall in short-term absence due to sickness, fewer headaches and increased concentration.

My friend Espen told me about his Finnish ex-manager, Pirkola. Espen thought Pirkola was cynical and authoritarian and found his presence unsettling. Their working relationship ended up becoming a real workplace conflict, and at one point Pirkola slammed his fist onto Espen's desk. He was angry and Espen was afraid. The environment at the office became toxic.

But then something happened and their strained relationship took an unexpected turn. A small banana plant had arrived in the office, and little did it know at the time what significance it would come to acquire. Both Espen and Pirkola became interested in this banana plant. They would bump into each other by it, each with their own watering can. Eventually they started talking about plants, bananas, light conditions ... and about this and that. They never became the best of friends, but the banana plant had acted as a tiny diplomat – it had got rid of some of the poisonous atmosphere in the workplace.

Studies have shown that green indoor plants can have a positive effect on the working environment, employee well-being and absence due to illness.

HANDY HINT

Want to be popular at work? Take over responsibility for the office plants. Everyone likes a colleague who uses plants to brighten up the place. I've tried it myself, and it works!

Urban green jungles around the world

It's not just my home country, Norway, that's seeing an increasing focus on the healing power of plants. There are always accounts popping up on Instagram, created by plant-lovers wanting to share their passion for plants. Everyone wants houseplants! Need more inspiration? Check these out:

@urbanjungleblog
Global inspo-source for houseplants. Mainly interiors and plants.

@homesteadbrooklyn
Resident in Brooklyn, USA. Has 800 potted plants and a chicken in her home.

@mamabotanica.amsterdam
From the Netherlands. An expert at cuttings and suckers.

@nikolicvladan
Mr. Houseplant – from Washington, USA. An incredibly knowledgeable plant enthusiast, who offers lots of practical advice and tips.

@plantpapis
A couple from Norway serving one part green aesthetic and one part helpful tips from their plant journey.

Off travelling? What about visiting a botanical garden? It's estimated that there are about 1,775 botanic gardens worldwide. Here are my Instagram-followers' favourites:

@kewgardens
Royal Botanic Gardens, Kew, London, England.

#singaporebotanicgardens
Singapore Botanic Gardens, Singapore.

@rbgedinburgh
Royal Botanic Garden, Edinburgh, Scotland.

@brooklynbotanic
Brooklyn Botanic Garden, New York City, USA.

@jardimbotanicorj
Jardim Botânico, Rio de Janeiro, Brazil.

@kirstenbosch.garden.official
Kirstenbosch National Botanical Garden, Cape Town, South Africa.

The Botanical Garden in Oslo.

PLANT PORTRAITS

The plant world is enormous! I have just 0.00025 per cent of the world's plant species. One hundred plants out of 390,900 known species makes my collection look modest and says something about how big the plant kingdom is. Here are my personal favourites, which I have found to be easy to get hold of and look after in Nordic conditions.

Aloe vera *Aloe vera*

A succulent that stores water in its leaves, aloe vera, is extremely robust. It can go for several months without access to water. Aloe vera isn't just beautiful and interesting to look at – the gel found inside the leaves also has proven medicinal properties and can alleviate mild skin irritations, such as sunburn and redness.

 LIGHT
Aloe vera enjoys a good, well-lit position, ideally in direct sunlight. It is accustomed to desert conditions, so give it as much sun as possible.

 WATERING
It needs extremely moderate watering. Aloe vera likes to dry out completely between waterings. It can usually be watered every other week, but sparingly. During winter, once a month will be enough.

SOIL
Use cactus and succulent compost with a layer of leca balls in the bottom. You can also use ordinary potting compost.

 FEEDING
This is an extremely frugal plant, so be stingy with the plant food. Give a little liquid organic plant food, or apply a specific fertilizer for succulents, once a month throughout spring and summer.

 ORIGIN
It is thought to come from Oman, though its origin is uncertain because merchants and mariners have taken it across the globe over the centuries due to its beneficial healing properties.

 MISCELLANEOUS
You can use the gel from the plant to soothe skin irritations. Aloe vera is a bit like a cucumber: it's 96 per cent water and it retains moisture exceptionally well. You can quite happily put an aloe vera outside during the summer – but give it a protected position beneath a roof so that you can control how much rainwater it gets. Note that aloe vera is mildly toxic to cats and dogs.

Areca palm *Dypsis lutescens*

The areca palm prompts thoughts of southern latitudes, sunshine and warmth. With its distinctive shape, it makes a lush, tropical feature in any home. In particular it is an air-purifier of some renown, making it a perfect plant for asthma- and allergy-sufferers. Studies have shown the areca palm to be a particularly effective cleanser of airborne toxins such as xylene and toluene (both VOCs found in paint thinners, for example).

LIGHT
The areca palm likes a well-lit position, ideally in bright, indirect light. A south-facing window is OK, but it shouldn't provide more than two to three hours of direct sunlight a day.

WATERING
It needs regular watering, when the top of the soil (the top few centimetres/about 1in) is dry. Water weekly during the warmer months, and a few times a month during the colder months. Water less in cooler rooms or where there is less light.

SOIL
Use potting compost with leca balls in the bottom of the pot. Areca palms are not demanding and do well in a small pot. If you want a large plant, repot every two or three years.

FEEDING
Feed with a liquid organic plant food two to three times a month during spring and summer. Give it little or no food in the colder months and for the first few months after repotting.

ORIGIN
It is native to Madagascar, where it can grow to 6 to 12m (20 to 40ft) in height.

MISCELLANEOUS
If given good growing conditions, it can occasionally put out panicles of small yellow flowers, which then develop into small, egg-shaped fruits. These start out yellowish in colour before maturing to a dark purple, almost black.

Because areca palms spread out at the top, they are ideal as room dividers, and they can be used to create zones and as screens, both at home and in the office.

Asparagus fern *Asparagus setaceus*

One of the most delicate and airy plants I know of
– the asparagus fern is magnificent and elegant at the
same time! Although it looks like a fern with its slender,
downy branches and a gossamer-like appearance, it is in
fact a member of the asparagus family. This is a plant that
loves moisture, so if you have a bathroom with a window
it will do extremely well there. Asparagus ferns lend
themselves to being free-standing eye-catchers, on
a sideboard or in a hanging pot.

LIGHT
The asparagus fern does well away from
the windows, and in indirect light. Keep
the plant out of direct sunlight, as it may
cause the fronds to turn yellow.

WATERING
It likes plenty of water – try not to let
the soil dry out. Keep damp at all times.

SOIL
Use potting compost with a layer of
leca balls at the bottom. You can also
mix a few leca balls in with the soil, for
particularly good drainage.

FEEDING
Feed with liquid organic plant food
once or twice a month during the
growing season.

ORIGIN
The asparagus fern originates from
South Africa.

MISCELLANEOUS
If the foliage turns yellow, it might be
a sign of too much warmth, too much
water or light that is too strong. About
18°C (64°F) is ideal. It's best to cut the
yellow foliage away – but be careful
when doing this as the branches have
small spurs that can prick. Note the
plant is toxic to pets. It is not considered
toxic for people, but the sap may cause
skin irritation.

Avocado plant *Persea americana*

This is a classic with the grow-it-yourself crowd! But to avoid disappointment, you shouldn't expect an avocado tree grown from a stone (see page 29) to produce fruit, as this takes at least five years in ideal conditions. But imagine the satisfaction of being able to look at an avocado plant that you've grown yourself while tucking into your Friday taco!

 LIGHT
This plant welcomes a sunny spot, and even a sheltered location outdoors during the summer.

 WATERING
It likes plenty of water – try not to let the soil dry out. Keep the soil moist at all times, but beware: yellow leaves are a sign of over-watering.

 SOIL
Use potting compost with a layer of leca balls at the bottom. You can also mix a few leca balls into the soil for a little extra drainage.

 FEEDING
Apply liquid organic plant food once or twice a month during the growing season.

 ORIGIN
The avocado probably originated from Mexico, though there is some scholarly debate on the subject.

 MISCELLANEOUS
Ever bought an unripe avocado from the shop? You can speed up the ripening process by putting it in a paper bag with a ripe banana. The plant is mildly toxic to pets.

Banana plant *Musa*

This is a classic, tropical plant that immediately creates associations with warmer climes – but be aware that it takes some effort to grow one successfully. The banana plant looks robust, but it has relatively brittle leaves despite their size. The variant that is usually sold in plant shops, 'Dwarf Cavendish', reaches half the height of its larger cousins, at between 1.8m and 3m (6ft and 10ft). Banana plants love moisture and warmth. They can be left out during the warmer months as long as they're in a sheltered position away from wind and draughts, as these can cause the leaves to tear. As the banana plant grows, the older leaves will develop brown tips that eventually turn yellow. This is entirely natural, and they can be removed, which will stimulate new growth.

 LIGHT

This a light-loving plant that does well in bright, indirect light, though avoid prolonged, scorching sunlight, especially when the plant is young and the leaves are still fresh. The ideal position is in a warm room, near to an east- or west-facing window. Ideally it should get 12 hours of daylight, so consider using a plant grow light for a top-up during the colder months.

 WATERING

It likes rather damp soil, but make sure that the top layer (a few centimetres/about 1in) is allowed to dry out between waterings. Water a few times a week during spring and summer – less in the winter, to prevent root rot.

 SOIL

Use ordinary potting compost, with a layer of leca balls in the bottom. You can also mix a few leca balls into the compost to ensure good drainage.

 FEEDING

Banana plants are quite greedy and like to be fed with a liquid organic plant food throughout spring and summer, ideally every other week.

 ORIGIN

The banana plant is native to South-east Asia, where it quickly grows to 2.5–5m (8–16ft).

 MISCELLANEOUS

Banana plants need spacious pots in order to grow taller. Repot annually during the first few years. As the plant gets older, it will start producing side shoots. These can be carefully removed from the parent plant (with as many roots as possible) and planted directly into new, nutritious soil. Banana plants can grow extremely quickly. With ideal growing conditions, new leaves can grow about 10cm (4in) a day.

Boston fern *Nephrolepis exaltata*

Ferns are moisture-loving plants that have excellent air-purifying properties. In the natural world ferns are sometimes considered a weed – bracken (*Pteridium*), for example, and a relation of the Boston fern, *Nephrolepis cordifolia* – but indoors their lush, rich green foliage can make them a real decorative asset. Boston ferns are available in many forms, including some with curly leaves (for example *N. exaltata* 'Emina' and 'Fluffy Ruffles'). In the wild, they grow on the forest floor where conditions are damp and shady.

 LIGHT
The Boston fern does well in the middle of a room and in the shade of other plants. It is happy in moderate light conditions.

 WATERING
A moisture-loving plant, it likes to be kept damp at all times. Water while the soil is still moist, but don't let it get soggy. Ferns also absorb water through their leaves. They like getting wet and being misted regularly.

 **SOIL**
Use ordinary potting compost with a layer of leca balls in the bottom. You can also mix a few leca balls into the compost to ensure good drainage.

 FEEDING
Apply a liquid organic plant food once a month from spring to autumn.

 ORIGIN
It is native to tropical regions worldwide.

 MISCELLANEOUS
Give the plant a shake now again to get rid of dead leaves.

Calamondin *Citrus x microcarpa*

This citrus fruit plant is readily available in most well-stocked plant shops. Whenever I post pictures of my 10-year-old calamondin on Instagram, I get a lot of comments from followers in the Philippines, where the fruit – and especially its juice – is used in cooking. Once the fruit is ripe, I usually challenge myself to eat one a day, for a quick blast of vitamin C – but they are incredibly sour! Note that the fruit is toxic to cats and dogs.

LIGHT
Calamondin likes good, sunny conditions – ideally direct sunlight. If you put it outside once the risk of frost has passed, make sure that it is in shade at first in order to avoid sun damage.

WATERING
It likes to dry out in between waterings, so water moderately. In spring and summer, water once or twice a week. During the winter, it goes into hibernation, and can be moved somewhere cool and slightly dark, with only occasional watering. If you have a loft or a basement, these are good storage options for when there are frosts at night.

SOIL
Use ordinary potting compost with a layer of leca balls in the bottom. You can also mix a few leca balls into the compost to ensure good drainage. There is also special low-calcium potting compost available, which is ideal for calamondin and other citrus fruits.

FEEDING
Use a liquid organic plant food once a month from spring until autumn.

ORIGIN
Calamondins are assumed to be from China, though they are now most commonly found in Indonesia and the Philippines, where the fruit is often used in food preparation.

MISCELLANEOUS
You can use the juice of calamondins just as you would use lime juice. It's ideal for use in marmalade or chutney. For my part, I think it's both fun and decorative to use the fruit as a garnish in a gin and tonic.

Calathea *Calathea orbifolia*

They say that beauty often comes at a price – and this luxuriant, vain plant with its striking foliage requires a lot of care and attention. Calatheas are recommended for those who like pottering with plants and who require a visual feast for the eye. They enjoy conditions on the jungle floor, where it's damp and there's little direct sunlight. As a result, they can cope with less light than a lot of other plants, and this makes them ideal houseplants. Calatheas do well in half shade, and ideally in damp conditions – for example in bathrooms with regular access to steam from baths and showers.

LIGHT
Calathea needs bright, indirect light, and can often cope well in shade. It does not tolerate direct sunlight and its leaves easily become sunburnt. Avoid moving the plant as much as possible.

WATERING
It loves moisture and requires quite a lot of watering – several times a week during the warmer months, once or twice a week during the colder months. However, don't leave it standing in water, as the roots will drown and rot. It likes damp air, so mist often.

SOIL
Use potting compost with a layer of leca balls in the bottom.

FEEDING
Feed with liquid organic plant food two to three times a month during the warmer months. Cut back feeding to once a month in the autumn, and none at all during winter.

ORIGIN
It is native to Latin America's tropical and subtropical forests.

MISCELLANEOUS
Calatheas are tropical and they like heat. If the temperature falls below 12°C (54°F), the leaves will curl up. Cutting away any yellow or brown leaves, preferably as far as the stem, will stimulate new growth. Pruning is not required, but remove any damaged or diseased leaves.

Calatheas have large, strong leaves and thrive in high humidity. They can be misted with lukewarm water a few times a week, and they will thank you if you stand them on a layer of leca balls or a foam brick with a few centimetres (about 1in) of water in the bottom. Other people swear by humidifiers, but ideally place them in a bathroom with a window, where the plant is regularly bathed in the steam from showers and baths.

Chinese money plant *Pilea peperomioides*

We have many names for the things we love – and this distinctive plant, in recent years the IT star of the plant world, is known as the Chinese money plant, pancake plant, UFO plant and missionary plant. With its long stems and beautiful round, dark-green leaves, the elegant Chinese money plant is the epitome of urban chic. It has long been popular in Scandinavia, thanks to its introduction from China by the Norwegian Agnar Espegren.

LIGHT
The Chinese money plant needs lots of light, so it can be placed directly in the window. Avoid direct sunlight during the summer, as this may damage the leaves.

WATERING
It likes high humidity and weekly watering during the warmer months. Go easy during the winter, when you should allow the soil to dry out between waterings.

SOIL
Use ordinary potting compost, but it will also do OK in seed or cactus and succulent compost. Give it good drainage, with holes in the bottom of the container, perhaps with some leca balls as a bottom layer.

FEEDING
Feed with a liquid organic plant food two to three times a month during the spring and summer. It needs little or no food during the winter months.

ORIGIN
Originally from Yunnan province in southern China, the Chinese money plant grows wild in damp forests at heights of 1,500–3,000m (5,000–10,000ft).

MISCELLANEOUS
In warmer months, it can flower in the form of large clusters of tiny yellow-green flowers. It is easy to propagate from suckers (see page 34).

Who hasn't dreamed of money growing on trees? A Chinese money plant won't make you rich, but perhaps, like Agnar Espegren, you will find out how you can make other people happy by giving them a baby *pilea* or two.

Emerald palm *Zamioculcas zamiifolia*

This is the plant for those wanting something that is tolerant, not fussy and easy to look after. The emerald palm can cope with most things and is the perfect beginner's plant for anyone who isn't at all green-fingered. It has decorative leaves that are large, thick and shiny – but the most fascinating thing is what we find beneath the soil: the large, potato-shaped, rhizome-like roots with a unique ability to store water. And that's why this plant is able to survive lengthy periods without watering – perfect for forgetful gardeners!

 LIGHT
The emerald palm can tolerate most things – from too much light to not enough. I have several of my own in my bathroom, where the only light is from the ceiling spots, and they're always putting out new growth. They seem to do well in relatively warm rooms.

 WATERING
It can cope with long dry periods, and prefers being forgotten and left to dry out rather than being over-watered.

 SOIL
Use seed, cactus or potting compost. For good drainage, add leca in the bottom of the pot and also mixed in with the soil. The emerald palm likes a crowded container. Don't repot until the roots look as if they'll burst out, and then to a pot that is only a few centimetres (1in) bigger in diameter.

 FEEDING
It generally needs only very little feeding. Feed with liquid organic plant food two to three times during the warmer months.

 ORIGIN
It is native to Africa, all the way from Kenya to South Africa.

 MISCELLANEOUS
Emerald palms can be easily propagated by splitting up the rootball and potting in fresh soil. The plant is an air-purifier and good for asthma- and allergy-sufferers. Note that the sap in the leaves contains oxalic acid, which can irritate mucous membrane.

False shamrock *Oxalis triangularis*

What makes this plant so popular is its beautiful dark purple leaves. For my part, I think it looks like a flock of butterflies – in shades of dark brown to burgundy – hence its other common name: butterfly sorrel. The leaves are sensitive to light conditions. They open up in the morning and close again when the sun goes down in the evening. The false shamrock is also a fantastic herb. It's reminiscent in flavour of the better-known wood sorrel (*Oxalis acetosella*), also a relative, and it has recently acquired a natural place in modern Nordic cuisine. It has a fresh and acidic taste, like a mixture of lemon and clover. Because the leaves contain oxalic acid, it's not recommended to be eaten in large quantities, especially if you have rheumatism or other inflammatory disorders. Note that it is toxic to pets.

 LIGHT
False shamrock needs good light conditions in order to stay healthy and vigorous. You can put it outdoors in the summer, but avoid direct sunlight.

 WATERING
It likes fairly moist soil, but make sure that the top layer of soil (a few centimetres/about 1in) dries out between each watering. The false shamrock is very forgiving, so if you do forget it and the plant looks dead, watering will revive the roots and new shoots will emerge.

 SOIL
Use ordinary potting compost with a layer of leca balls in the bottom. You can also mix a few leca balls into the compost to ensure good drainage.

 FEEDING
Feed with liquid organic plant food once a month during spring and summer. Give it little or no food during the winter months and also for the first few months after repotting.

 ORIGIN
It is native to tropical regions in Brazil and neighbouring countries in South America.

 MISCELLANEOUS
It likes to be repotted annually to stimulate growth. It's particularly rich in vitamin C and used to be eaten by sailors to prevent scurvy.

Fiddle-leaf fig *Ficus lyrata*

This decorative plant, with its photogenic appearance and exciting foliage, is the big Instagram hit of our times. The fiddle-leaf fig works well as an eye-catcher by itself in a big pot. It's relatively robust, as long as you don't move it around too much. So, find a good spot for it and leave it there. With really good indoor conditions, you can expect your fiddle-leaf fig to grow to 2m (6½ft) in height. It likes a good dusting now and again. The hard, slightly rigid leaves often attract airborne dust particles, so in order to help it get as much light as possible, use a slightly damp cloth to wipe the leaves down once in a while.

 LIGHT

The fiddle-leaf fig likes lots of bright, indirect light. It can tolerate some direct sunlight if placed in an east- or west-facing window (i.e. for shorter periods of morning or evening sun).

 WATERING

The fiddle-leaf fig likes to dry out between waterings. Use the finger trick to see if the plant needs water. If the soil is dry a few centimetres (about 1in) down into the pot, it's time to water.

 SOIL

Use ordinary potting compost with a layer of leca balls in the bottom. To ensure good drainage, mix a few leca balls in with the compost. The fiddle-leaf fig likes frequent repotting during the first few years, as this stimulates growth and gives the plant good conditions in which to grow.

 FEEDING

It is a fairly flexible plant when it comes to feeding. During the growing season, you can quite happily give it liquid organic plant food once a month.

 ORIGIN

The fiddle-leaf fig is native to West Africa, from Sierra Leone to Cameroon. In the wild, this plant can grow up to 15m (49ft) in height.

 MISCELLANEOUS

You can propagate a fiddle-leaf fig from cuttings. Remove a leaf from the top of the plant and put the cutting in water so that the stem can form roots. Be prepared for the fact that it can be rather challenging to get the cutting to put out roots. All the same, one of the advantages of taking a cutting from the top is that this will encourage the parent plant to bush out and form new branches. Fiddle-leaf fig is mildly toxic to children and pets.

Fig *Ficus carica*

This is one of my absolute favourites! A delicate, airy and elegant plant that gives any home a lush, green look, the fig immediately gives a Mediterranean feel. The fig has huge historic and cultural significance, not least that it is thought to be the biblical tree of life. If your fig tree has the ideal conditions, you can even grow your own soft, green and purple figs. In my experience, having tried to grow the fruit for several years, I can confirm that it's really difficult (in Norway) – except in record-breaking hot summers. But all is not lost – if you infuse fig leaves in cream you can use them to give your panna cotta a taste of fig. The fig tree is deciduous, so in the winter it will drop its leaves. Leave it to over-winter somewhere cool, but frost-free, with just a little light from a window. In spring, when new leaves appear, put the tree back in the living room or, as soon as the danger of frosts has passed, outdoors.

LIGHT
Figs prefer a warm, sunny corner.

WATERING
A thirsty plant that requires quite a lot of water, the fig tree also needs good drainage to allow any surplus water to drain out. During winter, when the plant is dormant, reduce watering to once a month.

SOIL
Use a generously sized pot with ordinary potting compost and with a layer of leca balls in the bottom. Make sure the pot is big enough for a few growing seasons as fig trees aren't so fond of being repotted.

FEEDING
It needs very little plant food, but give it some liquid organic plant food a few times during the growing season.

ORIGIN
They are native to South-east Asia and the Mediterranean region.

MISCELLANEOUS
Fig trees sometimes give off a rank smell. Although some people will suspect the cat, the real culprit is the fig tree lurking in the corner. Note that the fig tree is toxic to pets.

Fishbone cactus _Epiphyllum anguliger_

One of my recommendations for those of you who want
a robust plant, the fishbone cactus can withstand a lot
– just not direct sunlight. This unusual succulent with its
fern-like fronds thrives in a damp climate and half shade
– its natural home is the humid rainforest – whereas
most other succulents (and cacti) are parched sun-
worshippers. The fishbone cactus is particularly suited
to a hanging pot or being raised up on a pedestal where
its eye-catching, fishbone-shaped leaves are displayed to
full effect.

LIGHT
The fishbone cactus prefers half-shade,
so it can stand in places without
much light.

WATERING
Allow the soil to dry out completely
between watering. It likes a light
mist from a spray bottle, especially
when the indoor air is dry during the
colder months.

SOIL
Use a cactus and succulent compost
with a layer of leca balls in the bottom.
You can also mix a few balls in with
the soil for really good drainage.

FEEDING
Feed with liquid organic plant food a few
times during the warmer months.

ORIGIN
The fishbone cactus is native to Mexico.

MISCELLANEOUS
It can help to trim extremely long leaves,
or to cut them back completely. This
will stimulate the growth of fresh new
shoots.

Golden pothos *Epipremnum aureum*

This classic houseplant was almost obligatory in every home back in the 70s. Like the areca palm and mother-in-law's tongue, golden pothos has particularly good air-purifying properties. It's fairly hardy and robust, making it an easy plant to grow. It does well if allowed to wind around a moss pole, or shaped around the pot it's growing in. My partner has a golden pothos hanging from the ceiling in his apartment beneath a skylight, where it's doing really well. Although this is basically a tropical plant that loves warmth and moisture, it's so adaptable that it will usually be grateful for whatever indoor climate and care it's given. The leaves of the golden pothos are usually a plain, glossy green when grown as an indoor houseplant but, with ideal conditions and enough light, the leaves will develop their characteristic streaks and blotches in cream and yellow.

 LIGHT
This is not a fussy plant. Ideally give it bright, indirect light, but avoid direct sunlight as it will burn the tips of the leaves. It will survive a dark corner, but growth will be slow.

 WATERING
Water regularly, whenever the top few centimetres (about 1in) of soil are dry. Water weekly during the warmer months, and reduce to a few times a month during the colder months. Make sure the roots aren't left standing in damp soil, as they will rot.

 SOIL
Use potting compost with leca balls in the bottom. Golden pothos can happily be repotted every year or every other year, in order to stimulate further growth.

 FEEDING
Feed two to three times a month with liquid organic plant food during the warmer months. Give it little or no plant food during the winter. The same applies to the first few months after repotting.

 ORIGIN
Golden pothos orginates from Polynesia, where it grows as a creeper.

 MISCELLANEOUS
Even though golden pothos is perfect for asthma- and allergy-sufferers – thanks to its air-purifying properties – it's also poisonous, so it's never safe to chew or eat it.

Golden pothos is extremely easy to propagate. Take a cutting with two to four leaves attached and leave in water for a few weeks to put out roots or directly into moist soil. (See page 33 on propagation.)

Money plant/Jade plant *Crassula ovata*

A tree-like succulent that retains water in its leaves, the money plant can survive long dry periods. According to the ancient Chinese practice of Feng Shui, the money plant is considered a symbol of luck and good fortune, hence the name. This easy-going plant can survive for several months without access to water. Given ideal conditions, a mature plant may put out small, starry pink or white flowers during the spring.

LIGHT
The money plant requires plenty of sun – ideally direct sunlight – in order to grow properly. It is accustomed to desert conditions, so give it as sunny a position as possible. It can help to turn the plant regularly to ensure symmetrical growth.

WATERING
Water extremely moderately; the plant likes the top layer of soil to dry out completely between waterings. As a general rule, water sparsely every other week. Water just once a month during winter, but only when the soil in the pot has dried out completely.

SOIL
Use a 1:4 mix of horticultural sand to potting compost with a layer of leca balls in the bottom. You can also use ordinary potting compost mixed with some peat moss.

FEEDING
An extremely frugal plant, so be stingy with the plant food. Give the plant a little liquid organic plant food a few times during the warmer months.

ORIGIN
The money plant is native to South Africa.

MISCELLANEOUS
Money plants can be propagated from leaf cuttings (see page 30). Money plants can be repotted in the spring if the roots have become crowded. They do best in a relatively shallow pot. Note that the plant is toxic to pets, and mildly toxic to people. Contact may also cause skin irritation.

Mother-in-law's tongue *Sansevieria trifasciata*

This is a very robust succulent that can tolerate most things, including drying out and dry indoor winter air. It is also known as the bayonet plant due to its distinctive, sharp, thick leaves. Mother-in-law's tongue has a reputation as one of the best air-purifying plants there is, which makes it perfect for asthma- and allergy-sufferers. It magically converts carbon dioxide to oxygen, even at night, and for this reason it's often found in bedrooms. According to NASA, it would be possible for one person to live in a hermetically sealed bedroom if it contained six to eight mother-in-law's tongues. This may be true, but I suggest that you do not try this at home.

LIGHT
In its natural habitat, Mother-in-law's tongue often grows in direct sunlight and warmth, so prefers bright, direct sunlight in the home. However, it is a highly tolerant plant, and can also cope with lots of shade.

WATERING
Water infrequently – every three weeks in the spring and summer months, and no more than once a month the rest of the year. It prefers drying out and periods of neglect.

SOIL
Use seed, cactus or ordinary potting compost. If using potting compost, mix plenty of leca in with the soil to ensure good drainage. Mother-in-law's tongue likes a crowded pot, so avoid large pots. Don't repot until the roots look as if they're bursting out of the pot, and then to a pot that is only a few centimetres (about 1in) bigger in diameter.

FEEDING
It requires only a little food – once a month is enough during the warmer months. If it has just been repotted, the nutrients already present in the soil will usually last for a year. Otherwise you can apply slow-release plant food once a year.

ORIGIN
It is native to tropical West Africa where it is actually used to make rope because the leaf fibres are so tough.

MISCELLANEOUS
Mother-in-law's tongue can be propagated by cutting off a leaf and planting it directly in soil. Note that the plant is poisonous – including for our four-legged friends.

Rubber plant *Ficus elastica*

This handsome plant belongs to the fig family. Its leaves contain a milky fluid known as latex, which was formerly used in the production of rubber – hence the name. The rubber plant is extremely easy to look after and can put up with a lot. The only thing it doesn't like is over-watering and being moved around too much. The plant has attractive, shiny, leathery leaves that can benefit from a wipe with a damp cloth once a month in order to retain its sheen and to ensure optimal light uptake.

LIGHT
The rubber plant prefers good light conditions. If left in bright sunlight, the leaves will turn more burgundy-brown than green.

WATERING
Water regularly, whenever the top few centimetres (about 1in) of soil are dry. Water weekly during the warmer months, and a few times a month during the rest of the year. The darker and the cooler the room, the less water it needs.

SOIL
Use ordinary potting compost with a layer of leca balls in the bottom. For good drainage, you can mix some leca balls in with the soil. It's fine with repotting every other year and will happily share a large pot with other rubber plants.

FEEDING
Feed a few times a month with liquid organic plant food during spring and summer. Give it little or no plant food during the colder months.

ORIGIN
The rubber plant originates from India and Malaysia, where it can grow up to 40m (130ft) tall.

MISCELLANEOUS
Toxic to pets – and the sap in the leaves can cause skin irritations in people.

Spider plant *Chlorophytum comosum*

The spider plant is a rewarding plant which, as well as looking fresh and luxuriant with its apple-green colouring, also has good air-purifying properties. It is particularly suitable for growing in hanging pots or on a pedestal. The spider plant will do fine almost regardless of growing conditions, though it does take some care to get it to really thrive and provide you with small plantlets, or spiderettes, from the tips of long shoots. Left on the parent plant, spiderettes will in turn produce their own runners and plantlets, but they can also be removed and propagated.

 LIGHT
The spider plant likes half-shade or partial sunlight, but avoid direct sunlight as this will burn the tips of the leaves.

 WATERING
It likes regular moisture, but leave to dry out a little between waterings. Give it a light mist from time to time, especially when the indoor air is dry during the colder months.

 SOIL
Use ordinary potting compost with a layer of leca balls in the bottom. You can also mix leca balls in with the soil for really good drainage.

 FEEDING
Feed with liquid organic plant food a few times during the spring and summer months.

 ORIGIN
The spider plant is native to Southern Africa.

 MISCELLANEOUS
If you're looking for a hardy, green feature for your home, spider plants can also cope with low temperatures – even as low as 5°C (41°F) for a few weeks at a time (but they will not tolerate frost).

Swiss cheese plant/Monstera _Monstera deliciosa_

The Swiss cheese plant is the most widely grown member of the _Monstera_ genus. Do you remember the 70s? If you do, then you might have wearied of this ubiquitous exotic – the tropical plant _du jour_ of trendy living rooms and student digs everywhere. It has now made a comeback and paved the way for the houseplant trend of recent years. I was born in the 1980s, and I think it's a fantastic, fascinating and beautiful plant. This plant just doesn't give up. It is incredibly adaptable and tenacious – and perhaps that explains why it has become an ambassador for the new houseplant revolution? You see it everywhere, with its distinctive, large, heart-shaped leaves with their characteristic holes and slits – an adaptation that prevents the plant breaking in the heavy tropical rain showers of its home territory.

LIGHT
The Swiss cheese plant likes a lot of bright, indirect light. During the warmer months, move it slightly back from the sunniest window to prevent the leaves burning and turning brown, then move it nearer the window in the colder months.

WATERING
It needs regular moisture, whenever the top few centimetres of soil (about 1in) are dry. Water weekly during the warmer months, and reduce to a few times a month during the colder months. Water less in cooler rooms or where there is less light.

SOIL
Use ordinary potting compost with a layer of leca balls in the bottom. If you want a big plant, it can be repotted every year or every other year. The roots quickly become crowded.

FEEDING
Feed with a liquid organic plant food a few times a month during spring and summer. It requires little or no food during the winter months.

ORIGIN
The Swiss cheese plant originates from Southern Mexico, where it grows in humid rainforests.

MISCELLANEOUS
If the leaves do not split, this is a sign that it is not getting enough light. To stimulate new growth, try removing the lower, smaller leaves as the plant gets bigger. Note that it is toxic to people and pets.

It's so easy to get lost in these enormous Swiss cheese plants in the Estufa Fria greenhouse in Lisbon, Portugal. If you look closely, you can just make out the author's head amongst the sea of monstera.

Umbrella plant *Schefflera*

If you're looking for a loyal, friendly giant to add to your collection, this is the one to go for! The umbrella plant can reach 2.5m (8ft) tall or more and has modest needs, requiring only minimal care. It can even cope with temperatures down to 0°C (32°F) if accidently left outside in a sheltered spot. A perfect plant for forgetful owners.

 LIGHT
The umbrella plant likes as much light as possible, but avoid direct sunlight. During the winter, it may lose some leaves, but not too many if it has good light conditions.

 WATERING
It is happy to dry out between waterings. Give it a good soaking once the soil has completely dried out.

 SOIL
Use normal potting compost with a layer of leca balls in the bottom. You can also mix leca balls in with the soil for really good drainage.

 FEEDING
It needs little feeding, but give it some liquid organic plant food once a month throughout the growing season.

 ORIGIN
The umbrella plant is native to Taiwan, where it can grow up to 10m (33ft) tall in the wild.

 MISCELLANEOUS
It is one of the easiest plants to propagate. Either cut off the entire top, or just take a branch. Leave this in water in a clear bottle or a glass until you can see roots forming, then pot it up in compost. You can also try potting up a branch directly, as this will often root successfully. The plant is mildly toxic to people and pets. The sap in the stems and leaves can cause skin irritation.

Waxplant *Hoya*

Hoya is a plant genus of about 200–300 species. Most have waxy, slightly thick leaves. It's a keen climber that can wind a long way with the right support from steel or plant wire. The waxplant is known for having fairly modest requirements. Given ideal growing conditions, it will form attractive, porcelain-like flowers which have a strong scent, particularly in the evening.

 LIGHT
A waxplant should ideally get 12 hours of continuous light. It does fine in direct sunlight, but it doesn't like draughts and grows best at temperatures over 15°C (59°F).

 WATERING
It must be allowed to dry out between waterings. During spring and summer, it likes to be watered a few times a week, but much less frequently during autumn and winter.

 SOIL
Use ordinary potting compost with a layer of leca balls in the bottom. You can also mix a few leca balls into the compost to ensure good drainage.

 FEEDING
Feed with liquid organic plant food once a month from spring to autumn.

 ORIGIN
The waxplant orginates from forests in Australia and Asia.

 MISCELLANEOUS
To stimulate flowering, make sure you stand your waxplant in direct sunlight. The waxy flowers produce large drops of nectar – so watch out for sticky drips on your favourite table top! Note that the sap inside the leaves can be a skin irritant.

White bird of paradise *Strelitzia nicolai*

This big tropical plant is a distant relative of the banana plant, though it's easier to look after than its relation. The white bird of paradise can grow to 2m (6½ft) tall, even indoors. It has large, distinctive, grey-green leaves and can be fast-growing. In fact, it's not unusual for it to grow 10–15cm (4–6in) for each new leaf it puts out. The leaves of the white bird of paradise are brittle and tear easily, like those of the banana plant. This is nature's way of helping it withstand strong winds. I think it helps to give it even more of a tropical and decorative look. If you have an outdoor area or a balcony, this is a plant that likes to spend the warmer months outdoors.

 LIGHT
A light-loving plant, the white bird of paradise does well in good light conditions, though avoid prolonged periods in scorching sunlight. The ideal location is in a room close to an east- or west-facing window.

 WATERING
It likes fairly moist soil, but make sure that the top layer of soil (a few centimetres/about 1in) dries out between each watering. During spring and summer, water a few times a week. You could also use a damp cloth to wipe the leaves at regular intervals.

 SOIL
Use ordinary potting compost with a layer of leca balls in the bottom. You can also mix a few leca balls into the compost to ensure good drainage.

 FEEDING
Feed with liquid organic plant food ideally every other week during the spring and summer.

 ORIGIN
The white bird of paradise is native to South Africa, Madagascar and nearby countries in Africa.

 MISCELLANEOUS
Frequency of repotting will be dependent on how quickly the plant grows. During the first years, you can expect to have to repot each year, and then every other year. Side shoots can be separated off fairly easily, but not until the new plant has formed two or three leaves. If your white bird of paradise has extremely good growing conditions, it might produce exotic flowers that are reminiscent of a bird of paradise in flight. Note that it is mildly toxic to children and pets.

INDEX

INDEX OF COMMON NAMES

INDEX OF LATIN NAMES

SOURCES

Josifovic, Igor & De Graaff, Judith
Urban Jungle, Callwey Verlag, 2016

Langton, Caro & Ray, Rose
Et Hus med Planter, Cappelen Damm, 2018
also available in English
House of Plants, Frances Lincoln Publishers Ltd, 2016

Schilén, Linda
Älskade Krukväxter, Ordalaget Bokförlag, 2018

Stuber, Agnes
Krukväxter för Alla, Natur & Kultur, 2018

Vento, Susanna & Kantinkoski, Riikka
Green Home Book, Cozy Publishing, 2016

Viumdal, Jørn
Skoglufteffekten, Panta Forlag, 2018
also available in English
Skogluft: Forest Air, Harper Design, 2019

The Norweigan edition first published in 2019 by Cappelen Damm.

ISBN 978 82 02 61884 1
© Anders Røyneberg, 2019
Cappelen Damm AS.
www.cappelendamm.no
Published in agreement with
Northern Stories (All rights reserved)

Photography
pages 28 and 115:
@nelplant (Nelson De Coninck)
pages 66 and 123:
@annevaleur (Anne Valeur)
page 88:
@steffolsen (Steffen Olsen)
page 111:
@lillevinter (Weronica Melbø- Jørgensen)
All other photographs: Anders Røyneberg and Erik Schjerven

Specialist consultant Tommy Tønsberg
Design and layout Sissel Holt Boniface
Repro Narayana Press
Printing and binding Livonia Print, 2019, Latvia

This English Hardback edition published in 2021 by Quadrille.

First published in 2021 by Quadrille,
an imprint of Hardie Grant Publishing

Quadrille
52–54 Southwark Street
London SE1 1UN
quadrille.com

For the English language hardback edition:
Publishing Director Sarah Lavelle
Editor Stacey Cleworth
Copy-editor Jennifer Latham
Translation ArthemaxX Translation Agency
Designer Katherine Keeble
Head of Production Stephen Lang
Senior Production Controller Katie Jarvis

Cataloguing in Publication Data: a catalogue record for this book is available from the British Library.

Design and layout © Quadrille 2021

ISBN 978 1 78713 618 2

Printed in China

FSC
www.fsc.org
MIX
Paper from responsible sources
FSC™ C020056